Chapter 1: Introduction

Why Cash Flow Forecasting is Crucial

Cash flow forecasting is a vital business practice that involves predicting the amount of cash that will flow in and out of a company over a specific period. It is a powerful tool that can help businesses plan for future financial needs, identify potential cash shortages, and make informed business decisions. Effective cash flow forecasting can mean the difference between success and failure for any business, regardless of size or industry. The majority of businesses face cash flow issues at some point in their operations. In fact, according to a US Bank study, 82% of businesses fail due to poor cash flow management. This statistic highlights the importance of accurate and timely cash flow forecasting. Without it, businesses may be blindsided by unexpected expenses, fail to meet financial obligations, and ultimately struggle to survive.

The Benefits of Accurate Cash Flow Forecasting

Accurate cash flow forecasting offers numerous benefits for businesses. One of the most significant advantages is better financial management. With a clear understanding of future cash inflows and outflows, businesses can make informed decisions about spending, saving, and investing. This can lead to better cash flow management and improved profitability. Inaccurate cash flow forecasting can also lead to missed opportunities for growth and expansion. For example, if a company is expecting a large inflow of cash in the near future but fails to anticipate and plan for it, they may not have the necessary funds to take advantage of a promising investment opportunity. By accurately predicting future cash flows, businesses can make strategic decisions that can propel their growth and success.

An Overview of the 40 Strategies

In this book, we will delve into 40 different strategies for successful cash flow forecasting. These strategies cover a wide range of topics, including the basics of cash flow forecasting, data sources, forecasting techniques, managing cash flow during both growth and economic downturns, and specific strategies for different types of businesses and industries. We will also explore the importance of cash flow budgeting, cash flow timing strategies, and proactive cash management techniques. In addition, we will delve into the role of technology in cash flow forecasting, using financial ratios to analyze cash flow, and the benefits of scenario planning for cash flow management. Each chapter will offer valuable insights, practical tips, and real-world case studies to help readers understand and implement these strategies in their own businesses. Whether you are a small business owner, a financial professional, or someone looking to improve your personal financial management skills, these strategies will provide valuable guidance and techniques to help you effectively forecast and manage cash flow.

Now that we have provided an overview of the crucial role of cash flow forecasting and the benefits of accurate predictions, let's dive into the 40 strategies that can help businesses achieve success in this critical aspect of financial management.

Chapter 2: Understanding Cash Flow

When it comes to running a successful business, there are many factors that play a crucial role. From managing expenses to generating profits, there are various areas that need to be carefully monitored and controlled. However, one aspect that is often overlooked or misunderstood is cash flow. In Chapter 2, we will delve deeper into the concept of cash flow, its types, and its importance in running a successful business.

Definition of Cash Flow

Before we dive into the intricacies of cash flow, let's first understand what it means. In simple terms, cash flow refers to the amount of cash coming in and going out of a business during a specified period of time. This includes cash received from sales, investments, loans, and other sources, as well as cash paid for expenses, investments, and loans.

However, cash flow is not just limited to physical cash. It also includes the flow of funds in and out of a business's bank accounts, credit card transactions, and other forms of electronic payments. Essentially, any movement of funds into or out of a business is considered a part of cash flow.

Types of Cash Flow

There are three main types of cash flow: operating, investing, and financing. It is important for business owners to understand and track each type in order to gain a complete picture of their financial health.

Operating Cash Flow:
This refers to the cash flow generated from a business's day-to-day operations, such as sales, inventory purchases, and payments to suppliers. It is a crucial aspect of a business's financial health as it shows the company's ability to generate cash from its primary activities.

Investing Cash Flow:
Investing cash flow refers to the purchase or sale of long-term assets, such as property, equipment, or investments. It is the cash flow related to changes in a business's fixed assets.

Financing Cash Flow:
This type of cash flow is related to the funding of a business's operations through borrowing or equity financing. It includes cash received from loans, equity investments, or payments to shareholders.

Importance of Cash Flow in Business

Cash flow is often described as the lifeblood of a business. Without adequate cash flow, a company can struggle to pay its bills, cover its expenses, and ultimately survive. Therefore, understanding and managing cash flow is crucial for the success of any business. First and foremost, cash flow helps in keeping track of how much money is available for a business to use. By monitoring cash inflows and outflows, business owners can make informed decisions about spending and investments, ensuring that they have enough cash to cover their expenses. Additionally, cash flow analysis can also reveal potential problems or opportunities for a business. For example, if a business is consistently experiencing negative cash flow, it may indicate that expenses need to be cut or sales need to be increased. On the other hand, if the business has excess cash, it could mean that the company has room for growth or expansion. Moreover, cash flow forecasting can provide valuable insights for making future financial decisions. It can help businesses plan for periods of low cash flow, allowing them to proactively manage their finances. This can include negotiating better terms with suppliers, delaying non-essential purchases, or seeking additional financing options.

In conclusion, cash flow is a critical aspect of running a successful business. By understanding its definition, types, and importance, business owners can gain a better understanding of their financial health and make informed decisions for the future. In the next chapter, we will explore the basics of cash flow forecasting and how it can benefit a business.

Chapter 3: Understanding the Cash Flow Forecasting Process

Cash flow forecasting is an essential tool for businesses of all sizes and industries. It allows organizations to plan and manage their finances effectively and make more informed decisions. In this chapter, we will dive deeper into the cash flow forecasting process, the elements that make up a cash flow forecast, and the common tools used for cash flow forecasting.

Cash Flow Forecasting Process

The cash flow forecasting process involves analyzing and predicting the flow of cash in and out of a business over a specific period. It is a crucial aspect of financial planning as it helps businesses anticipate potential cash shortages or surpluses and take suitable action to mitigate any risks. The first step in the process is to gather all relevant financial data, including historical cash flow statements, accounts receivable, accounts payable, and inventory reports. This data will serve as the foundation for your cash flow forecast. Next, you need to establish a time horizon for your forecast. Typically, businesses forecast their cash flow on a monthly basis for the next 12 to 18 months. However, this may vary depending on the size and nature of the organization. Once you have gathered the data and established a time horizon, it is time to start creating your cash flow forecast. This involves projecting your cash inflows and outflows based on historical trends, market conditions, and any other factors that may impact your business's financials. While creating your cash flow forecast, it is essential to consider different scenarios and their potential impact on your cash flow. For example, what would happen if there is a sudden increase in customer demand or a decrease in sales? By considering various scenarios, you can plan for potential risks and make better-informed decisions.

As with any financial planning process, it is crucial to regularly monitor and update your cash flow forecast. This will help you track your actual cash flow against your projected cash flow and make necessary adjustments.

Elements of a Cash Flow Forecast

A cash flow forecast consists of three primary elements: operating activities, investing activities, and financing activities. Let's take a closer look at each of these elements:

1. Operating Activities:
These activities involve the day-to-day operations of the business, such as sales, payments to suppliers, and payroll. It is essential to accurately forecast these activities as they have a direct impact on your business's working capital and cash flow.

2. Investing activities:
These activities involve any purchases or sales of assets, such as equipment and property. It is crucial to consider any potential capital expenditures while creating your cash flow forecast, as these activities can significantly impact your cash flow.

3. Financing activities:
This element involves any borrowing or repayment of debt, as well as any equity financing. It is vital to monitor your financing activities carefully and incorporate them into your forecast, as they can have a significant impact on your business's cash flow and overall financial health.

Common Tools Used for Cash Flow Forecasting

With the advancement of technology, there are now several tools available to help businesses with cash flow forecasting. These tools range from simple spreadsheets to sophisticated software programs. Let's take a look at some of the most commonly used tools:

1. Spreadsheets:
Many businesses still use spreadsheets, such as Microsoft Excel, for cash flow forecasting. Spreadsheets are relatively easy to use and can be customized to suit individual business needs. However, they can be time-consuming, prone to human error, and lack advanced features and capabilities.

2. Accounting software:
Most accounting software programs, such as QuickBooks and Xero, come equipped with cash flow forecasting capabilities. These programs are designed specifically for

financial management and offer features like automation, real-time data updates, and advanced reporting.

3. Cash flow forecasting software:
There are also specialized software programs solely dedicated to cash flow forecasting. These programs offer more advanced features and capabilities, such as scenario planning and automated forecasting. However, they can be quite expensive and may require a learning curve to use effectively. Regardless of the tool you choose, it is crucial to select one that fits your business's needs and budget and allows for easy monitoring and updating of your cash flow forecast.

In conclusion, cash flow forecasting is a dynamic and continuous process that allows businesses to plan and manage their finances effectively. By understanding the cash flow forecasting process, the key elements of a cash flow forecast, and the available tools, businesses can gain better control of their cash flow and make more informed financial decisions. In the next chapter, we will explore the importance of a cash flow budget in the cash flow forecasting process.

Chapter 4: Why Use a Cash Flow Budget

Why Use a Cash Flow Budget

Creating and managing a cash flow budget is an essential task for any business, big or small. A cash flow budget is a financial document that outlines the expected inflows and outflows of cash for a specific period. It allows you to track the movement of cash in and out of your business, and helps you make informed decisions about your cash flow management. Here are some reasons why using a cash flow budget is crucial to the success of your business.

Components of a Cash Flow Budget

A well-prepared cash flow budget is made up of three key components: projected inflows, projected outflows, and the resulting cash balance. These components work together to provide a clear picture of your business' financial health. Let's look at each component in more detail.

Projected Inflows:
This component includes all the possible sources of cash for your business, such as sales revenue, loans, and investments. It is essential to have an accurate estimate of your expected cash inflows to create a realistic budget.

Projected Outflows:
This component covers all the expected cash outflows of your business, including expenses, loan payments, and dividends. It is crucial to consider both fixed and variable expenses when creating a cash flow budget to account for unexpected costs.

Resulting Cash Balance:
The resulting cash balance is the difference between your projected inflows and outflows. This component helps you to see if your business will have enough cash to cover its expenses and identify potential cash flow challenges.

Creating an Effective Cash Flow Budget

To create an effective cash flow budget, you need to follow a few key steps. Here are some tips to help you create a robust budget for your business.

1. Estimate Inflows and Outflows:
Take the time to carefully estimate all your expected inflows and outflows for the budget period. Use historical data, market trends, and industry insights to make informed projections.

2. Include All Sources of Cash:
Don't forget to include all the possible sources of cash, such as accounts receivable, lines of credit, and investment income. Try to be as comprehensive as possible to create an accurate budget.

3. Monitor Cash Flow Regularly:
Creating a budget is not a one-time task; it requires constant monitoring and updates. Compare your actual cash flow to your budget regularly and make adjustments as needed.

4. Plan for Contingencies:
Unexpected events can have a significant impact on your business's cash flow. It's crucial to plan for contingencies in your budget, such as an increase in expenses or a decrease in sales.

5. Consider the Timing of Cash Flows:
The timing of cash inflows and outflows can significantly impact your business' cash flow. Account for the timing of payments, such as when your customers pay their invoices or when you need to make loan payments.

6. Use Technology:
There are many cash flow budgeting tools available that can help you create and monitor your budget more efficiently. Consider using technology to streamline your budgeting process and get a more accurate picture of your cash flow.

In conclusion, a cash flow budget is a crucial tool for any business looking to stay financially healthy. It provides insight into your business's financial stability, helps you plan for the future, and allows you to make informed decisions about your cash flow management. By following these tips and creating a realistic and comprehensive budget, you can ensure the financial success of your business.

Chapter 5: Cash Flow Forecasting Techniques

Bottom-Up Forecasting

Bottom-up forecasting is a cash flow forecasting technique that involves breaking down the cash flow forecast into smaller components, such as individual departments or business units, and then aggregating them to obtain an overall forecast. This approach starts from the bottom of the organization and works its way up to the top. One of the key benefits of bottom-up forecasting is its accuracy. By involving departments and individuals directly responsible for expenses and revenues, the forecast is more likely to reflect the realities of the business. This approach also allows for a more detailed analysis of cash inflows and outflows, which can help identify areas where cost-cutting measures can be implemented. However, bottom-up forecasting can be time-consuming and resource-intensive. It requires input and collaboration from multiple departments, making coordination and communication crucial. This approach may also present challenges in aligning departmental forecasts with the overall financial goals of the organization.

To mitigate these challenges, it is essential to have a clear process for collecting and consolidating departmental forecasts. This process should also include regular check-ins and updates to ensure that the forecasts remain accurate and aligned with business objectives.

Top-Down Forecasting

In contrast to bottom-up forecasting, top-down forecasting starts with an overall estimate or projection of cash flow and then breaks it down into smaller components. This approach is often used by senior management to forecast cash flow for the organization as a whole. The benefit of top-down forecasting is that it provides a quick and high-level view of cash flow, allowing for a faster decision-making process. It is also less resource-intensive, as it does not require input from multiple departments. This approach is particularly useful for large organizations with complex cash flow operations.

However, top-down forecasting may lack accuracy due to its broad scope. It may miss important details and nuances that can affect cash flow projections. To address this, it is essential to have a thorough understanding of the business and its key drivers to ensure that top-down forecasts are based on informed assumptions.

Rolling Forecasting

Rolling forecasting is a continuous and iterative approach where the cash flow forecast is updated regularly to reflect any changes in the business environment. This technique is based on the premise that the accuracy of a forecast decreases over time, and updates are needed to maintain its relevance. The advantage of rolling forecasting is that it allows for flexibility and adaptability to changes in the business environment. This technique is especially useful for businesses that experience fluctuating cash flows or those operating in dynamic industries. However, rolling forecasting may present challenges in measuring performance and progress. With constantly changing forecasts, it is crucial to track and compare the accuracy of previous forecasts to avoid overestimating or underestimating cash flow. It is also essential to have a clear process for updating and communicating new forecasts to relevant parties.

In conclusion, a combination of these cash flow forecasting techniques may be more effective than relying on just one. For example, incorporating bottom-up forecasting for detail and accuracy, top-down forecasting for speed and efficiency, and rolling forecasting for flexibility and adaptability can result in a more comprehensive and realistic cash flow forecast. It is essential to consider the specific needs and characteristics of your business to determine which combination of techniques will work best for you.

Chapter 6: Data Sources for Cash Flow Forecasting

Forecasting cash flow is not just about looking at numbers and making predictions. It requires a deep understanding of your business, its operations, and the factors that can impact your cash flow. One of the key components of cash flow forecasting is data — gathering and analyzing relevant data to generate accurate predictions and make informed decisions. In this chapter, we will explore the various internal and external data sources that can be used for cash flow forecasting and how to use them effectively.

Internal Sources

Internal data sources are the data that is generated from within your organization, including your financial and accounting records. These data sources are often the most reliable and relevant for cash flow forecasting, as they provide a clear picture of your business's current financial situation. Here are some examples of internal data sources that can be used for cash flow forecasting:

Financial Statements

Your financial statements, including your balance sheet, income statement, and cash flow statement, are a vital source of data for cash flow forecasting. They show your company's historical financial performance, which can be helpful in predicting future cash inflows and outflows. It is essential to keep these statements updated and accurate to generate reliable forecasts.

Accounts Receivable and Accounts Payable Records

Your accounts receivable records show the amount of money that your customers owe you, while your accounts payable records show the amount of money that you owe to your suppliers. These records can help you anticipate when you can expect to receive payments and when you need to make payments, respectively, to manage your cash flow effectively.

Sales Data

Your sales data can provide valuable insights into your cash flow forecasting. By tracking your sales trends, you can estimate your future cash inflows and plan for any expected changes in demand. You can also use this data to compare your actual sales with your forecasted sales to make adjustments to your forecast as needed.

External Sources

External sources refer to the data that you gather from outside your organization. These sources can provide valuable information to help you understand market trends, economic conditions, and industry-specific factors that can impact your cash flow. Here are some examples of external data sources that you can use for cash flow forecasting:

Market Trends and Economic Data

Tracking market trends and economic data can help you understand your industry's current and future environment. For example, if interest rates are expected to increase, it may impact your ability to borrow funds, which can affect your cash flow. By keeping track of these external factors, you can make more accurate financial forecasts.

Industry Benchmarks and Key Performance Indicators (KPIs)

Comparing your company's performance against industry benchmarks and KPIs can provide valuable insights into your cash flow forecasting. These measures can help you understand how your business is performing compared to your competitors and the overall industry. They can also identify areas for improvement and assist in setting realistic financial goals.

Customer and Supplier Data

Your customers and suppliers can also provide valuable data for cash flow forecasting. By understanding their payment habits and patterns, you can better forecast your inflows and outflows. For example, if you have a customer who consistently pays late, you can adjust your forecast to account for potential delays in cash inflows.

How to Use Data to Generate Accurate Forecasts

Having access to reliable data is only the first step in generating accurate cash flow forecasts. The real challenge lies in analyzing and interpreting this data to make informed predictions. Here are some tips for using data to generate accurate cash flow forecasts:

Use Multiple Data Sources

To get a complete and accurate picture of your business's financial health, it is crucial to use data from both internal and external sources. Combining data from various sources can provide a more comprehensive understanding of your business and the factors that can impact your cash flow.

Regularly Update and Review Data

Data is only as useful as its accuracy and timeliness. It is essential to update and review your data regularly to ensure that your forecasts are based on the most recent and correct information. This can help you avoid making decisions based on outdated or incorrect data.

Be Mindful of Biases

When analyzing data, it is crucial to be mindful of any biases that may affect your interpretation. Confirmation bias, for example, can lead you to seek out and interpret data that supports your existing beliefs, leading to inaccurate forecasts. It is important to approach data with an open mind and consider all the facts.

Use Technology to Your Advantage

In today's digital world, there are various tools and software available to help you analyze and interpret data for cash flow forecasting. These tools can help you generate more accurate forecasts more efficiently, leaving you more time to focus on other aspects of your business.

Regularly Compare and Adjust Forecasts

Cash flow forecasting is not a one-time activity. Your forecasts should be regularly reviewed and compared to your actual cash flow to identify any discrepancies. If there are significant differences, adjust your forecasts accordingly to generate more accurate predictions for the future.

By understanding and effectively utilizing data from various sources, you can generate more accurate cash flow forecasts and make informed decisions for your business. In the next chapter, we will discuss in detail the different techniques for cash flow forecasting and how to choose the most suitable one for your business.

Chapter 7: Forecasting Inflows

Cash flow forecasting is a crucial aspect of financial management that involves predicting the amount of cash that will flow in and out of a business over a specific period of time. Inflows refer to any form of cash coming into the business, such as sales revenue, investments, loans, or other sources. Accurately forecasting your inflows is essential for maintaining the financial health of your business and ensuring that you have enough cash to cover your expenses. In this chapter, we will explore various methods for estimating future inflows, strategies for managing inflows effectively, and ways to improve collection times.

Methods for Estimating Future Inflows

Forecasting inflows can be a challenging task, especially for small businesses with limited resources. However, there are several methods that you can use to estimate your future inflows with a reasonable degree of accuracy. One common approach is to use historical data to identify patterns and trends in your cash inflows. By analyzing your past sales and receivables, you can make informed predictions about future inflows. Another method for estimating future inflows is to conduct market research and analyze industry trends. This approach is particularly useful for businesses that are just starting or those that are expanding into new markets. By understanding market conditions and customer behaviors, you can make more accurate predictions about your future inflows.

Additionally, you can use forecasting tools and software to help you with your inflow estimates. These tools use algorithms and data analysis to provide more accurate and sophisticated predictions. They also allow you to input different scenarios and variables, such as changes in sales or market conditions, to see how they affect your inflows.

Strategies for Managing Inflows

Once you have estimated your future inflows, the next step is to develop strategies for managing them effectively. The ultimate goal is to optimize your cash inflows to ensure that you have enough liquidity to cover your expenses and investment needs. One effective strategy for managing inflows is to incentivize early payments from customers. This can be done by offering discounts to customers who pay their invoices early or implementing a penalty for late payments. You can also consider implementing an online payment system to make it easier for customers to pay promptly. Another strategy is to diversify your sources of inflow. This means not relying on one big customer for the majority of your revenue, as this can be risky if that customer faces financial challenges. By having a diverse customer base, you can ensure a more stable cash inflow and reduce the risk of serious repercussions if one customer defaults.

Improving Collection Times

The speed at which you collect your receivables has a significant impact on your cash flow. The longer it takes for customers to pay, the longer you have to wait to have that cash available for your use. Therefore, it is crucial to have efficient and timely collection processes in place to improve your collection times. One strategy is to send out invoices promptly and regularly follow up with customers who have not yet paid. This ensures that customers are aware of their payment obligations and keeps you on their radar. You can also consider offering discounts to customers who pay their invoices within a certain timeframe to encourage timely payments.

Another way to improve collection times is to maintain good relationships with your customers. When you have a positive and professional relationship with your customers, they are more likely to prioritize paying their invoices promptly. This means maintaining good communication, providing excellent customer service, and addressing any disputes or issues promptly and respectfully.

In Conclusion

In conclusion, accurately forecasting your cash inflows and managing them effectively is crucial for the success of your business. By using appropriate methods for estimating future inflows, implementing strategies for managing inflows, and improving collection times, you can ensure a healthy cash flow and maintain the financial stability of your business. Remember to regularly review and update your cash flow forecast to adapt to changing market conditions and maintain control over your inflows.

Chapter 8: Managing Outflows for Successful Cash Flow Forecasting

Managing Fixed vs. Variable Costs

When it comes to managing outflows, it's important to understand the difference between fixed and variable costs. Fixed costs are expenses that remain constant regardless of the volume of sales or production. These can include rent, insurance, and salaries. On the other hand, variable costs are expenses that change based on the amount of sales or production. Examples of variable costs are raw materials, inventory, and commission fees. When forecasting your cash flow, it's crucial to accurately identify which costs are fixed and which are variable. This allows you to predict your cash outflows more accurately and make strategic decisions to improve your cash flow. By minimizing your fixed costs and focusing on controlling your variable costs, you can optimize your cash flow and make better financial decisions for your business.

Minimizing Outflows

One of the most effective ways to manage outflows is by implementing cost-cutting measures. This doesn't necessarily mean cutting essential expenses, but rather finding ways to reduce costs without compromising the quality of your products or services. Some helpful strategies include negotiating with vendors for better prices, streamlining processes to increase efficiency, and exploring alternative suppliers. Another way to minimize outflows is by regularly reviewing your expenses and identifying any unnecessary or non-essential costs. By eliminating these expenses, you can free up more cash for other important aspects of your business.

Predicting and Planning for Seasonal Fluctuations

Seasonal fluctuations can significantly impact your cash flow and cause unexpected cash shortages. For businesses that experience a change in demand based on the season, it's crucial to plan and prepare for these fluctuations. To accurately forecast cash flow during seasonal changes, it's essential to keep detailed records and analyze past data. This will help you identify patterns and trends in sales, allowing you to make more accurate cash flow projections. It's also important to plan for any additional expenses that may arise during peak seasons, such as increased marketing or hiring seasonal staff. Furthermore, having a plan in place to handle any cash shortages during slower seasons can help you avoid cash flow problems. This may include cutting back on non-essential costs or utilizing lines of credit or business loans to bridge the gap.

Saving for Unexpected Expenses

No matter how well you plan and manage your cash flow, unexpected expenses can still arise. This is why it's crucial to have a contingency plan and to save for unexpected outflows. By setting aside a portion of your profits each month, you can build up a cushion to cover unexpected expenses without disrupting your cash flow. Another helpful strategy is to regularly review and update your cash flow projections. This will help you identify any potential cash shortfalls in advance and plan accordingly.

Conclusion

Successfully managing outflows is an essential aspect of effective cash flow forecasting. By understanding the difference between fixed and variable costs, minimizing expenses, and planning for seasonal fluctuations and unexpected expenses, you can optimize your cash flow and make better financial decisions for your business. Regularly reviewing and updating your cash flow projections will also help you identify any potential problems and make adjustments to keep your cash flow on track. Remember, proper outflow management is crucial for maintaining a healthy and sustainable cash flow for your business.

Chapter 9: Managing Cash Flow Timing: Strategies for Success

Managing cash flow timing is crucial for any business. As the saying goes, "cash is king". Even profitable businesses can struggle due to poor management of cash flow timing. In this chapter, we will explore the impact of payment terms on cash flow and share strategies for accelerating inflows and delaying outflows. By mastering this aspect of cash flow forecasting, businesses can ensure stable cash flow and make informed financial decisions.

Managing Timing Differences

Timing differences can often cause major disruptions in cash flow. This happens when there is a gap between when money is received and when it is spent. For example, a business may have a large purchase to make, but their revenue will not be coming in until the following month. This can result in a shortage of cash and potentially lead to missed opportunities or even financial difficulties. The key to managing timing differences is to plan ahead and anticipate potential gaps in cash flow. One strategy is to create a cash reserve to cover any anticipated timing differences. Another approach is to closely monitor payment terms and adjust them accordingly. By understanding the timing differences in your business, you can proactively manage cash flow and avoid any potential shortages.

Impact of Payment Terms on Cash Flow

Payment terms play a significant role in managing cash flow timing. Businesses must strike a balance between receiving payments from customers and making payments to suppliers. The longer the payment terms are, the longer the business has to receive and use the money. However, this can also result in delayed payments from customers, causing potential cash flow issues. One strategy for managing payment terms is to negotiate favorable terms with suppliers. This can include negotiating for extended payment terms, discounts for early payments, or even setting up a payment schedule that aligns with your business's cash flow. Moreover, businesses can incentivize customers to pay early by offering discounts or other perks. By managing payment terms effectively, businesses can improve cash flow timing and maintain healthy finances.

Strategies for Accelerating Inflows and Delaying Outflows

In addition to managing payment terms, businesses can use other strategies to accelerate inflows and delay outflows. For example, offering discounts to customers who make full payments upfront can speed up cash flow. Another effective method is to review and renegotiate contracts with suppliers to extend the payment terms and delay outflows. Additionally, businesses can explore alternative financing options to cover short-term cash needs, such as invoice factoring or lines of credit. In today's digital age, technology can also be leveraged to accelerate inflows and delay outflows. For instance, implementing online payment systems can speed up customer payments by providing convenient and secure ways to make transactions. Furthermore, automating payment processes can save time and reduce the risk of human error, resulting in faster cash inflows and more efficient use of resources. Lastly, businesses can also consider implementing lean inventory management practices to delay outflows and optimize cash flow. By accurately forecasting demand and carefully managing inventory levels, businesses can reduce excess inventory and minimize the cost of goods sold. This reduces the amount of cash tied up in inventory, freeing it up for other purposes such as investments or short-term needs.

In Conclusion

Managing cash flow timing is critical for the success of any business. By understanding and actively managing timing differences, payment terms, and using various strategies to accelerate inflows and delay outflows, businesses can ensure stable and healthy cash flow. Additionally, leveraging technology and implementing efficient processes can also improve cash flow timing and help businesses make informed financial decisions. With effective cash flow timing management, businesses can avoid any potential financial challenges and focus on growth and profitability.

Chapter 10: Managing Cash Flow Strategies for Success

In this chapter, we will discuss the essential steps for managing your business's cash flow. As the saying goes, "cash is king," and it is crucial to have a solid understanding of your cash flow and how to effectively manage it. We will explore the best practices for managing working capital, strategies for cash flow management, and how to deal with unexpected changes in cash flow.

Managing Working Capital

Working capital is a key measure of a company's financial health. It represents the difference between current assets and current liabilities. Proper management of working capital is essential to ensure smooth operations and avoid financial troubles. The first step in managing working capital is to understand your cash conversion cycle, which is the amount of time it takes for a company to convert current assets into cash. Monitoring this cycle and finding ways to improve it can significantly impact cash flow. Next, it is crucial to review your inventory management processes. Keeping excessive inventory ties up your working capital and increases the risk of obsolescence. It is essential to find the balance between having enough inventory to meet demand and minimizing excess. In addition to inventory management, it is necessary to evaluate your accounts receivable and payable processes. Long receivable periods can strain cash flow, while short payable periods can put a strain on suppliers and relationships. It is vital to have an efficient collection process for accounts receivable and negotiate favorable payment terms with your suppliers.

Cash Flow Management Strategies

Effective cash flow management is crucial for the success of any business. It involves planning and managing your cash inflows and outflows to ensure there is always enough cash on hand to cover any financial obligations. Here are some strategies for managing cash flow:

- Create a cash flow forecast: This is a projection of your business's future cash flow based on your expected income and expenses. It can help you identify potential cash shortages and plan accordingly.

- Negotiate payment terms: It is essential to negotiate favorable payment terms with your suppliers to align with your cash flow forecast. This can include extending your payment terms or negotiating discounts for early payment.

- Monitor and control expenses: Regularly reviewing your expenses and identifying areas where you can cut costs can help improve your overall cash flow. Be mindful of unnecessary expenses and avoid overspending.

- Implement a cash reserve: Setting aside a portion of your profits as a cash reserve is a wise decision. It can act as a buffer during lean times and help avoid taking on debt or seeking external financing.

Dealing with Unexpected Changes in Cash Flow

As much as we try to forecast and plan for our cash flow, unexpected changes and disruptions can occur. It is essential to have a contingency plan in place for such situations. Here are some tips for dealing with unexpected changes in cash flow:

- Review and revise your budget: In the instance of a negative cash flow, it is crucial to review and revise your budget to reduce expenses and reallocate resources to focus on high-return activities.

- Cut discretionary spending: When facing cash flow disruptions, it is necessary to cut back on expenses that are not essential to your operations. This can include delaying new investments or decreasing non-crucial expenses.

- Consider financing options: In some cases, seeking external financing may be necessary to overcome cash flow challenges. This can include a business line of credit or a loan.

- Communicate with stakeholders: It is crucial to keep your stakeholders informed of any changes in cash flow and how it may impact the business. Transparency and communication can help build trust and support during tough times.

In conclusion, effective cash flow management is crucial for the success and sustainability of any business. By implementing the strategies discussed in this chapter and being prepared to navigate unexpected changes in cash flow, you can maintain a healthy cash flow and secure the financial stability of your business.

Chapter 11: Utilizing Technology for Accurate Cash Flow Forecasting

Using Technology to Improve Forecasting Accuracy

In today's fast-paced business world, manual methods of cash flow forecasting are simply not enough to effectively manage cash flow. With constantly changing market conditions and the need for quick decision making, companies need to rely on technology to improve the accuracy and efficiency of their cash flow forecasting. One of the key benefits of using technology for cash flow forecasting is the ability to access real-time data. With automated systems, businesses can track their cash flow in real-time, allowing for more accurate predictions of future cash flow. This eliminates the guesswork and potential errors that come with manual forecasting methods. Technology also offers advanced analytical tools that can help businesses better understand their cash flow patterns and make informed decisions. With features such as trend analysis, businesses can identify patterns and make adjustments to their forecasting strategies accordingly. In addition, technology can also help with scenario planning. With the ability to run multiple scenarios and simulations, businesses can predict the impact of potential changes in the market or their operations on cash flow. This allows for more proactive and strategic decision making.

Common Cash Flow Forecasting Software

There is a wide range of cash flow forecasting software available, each with its own unique features and capabilities. Some of the most commonly used software include:

1. QuickBooks

QuickBooks is a popular accounting software that also offers cash flow forecasting capabilities. It integrates with bank accounts and credit cards, making it easy to track and predict cash flow. It also has a user-friendly interface, making it accessible for businesses of all sizes.

2. Cashflow Manager

Another popular choice for cash flow forecasting, Cashflow Manager offers a range of tools and features for businesses to effectively manage their cash flow. Some of its key features include automated bank feeds, budgeting and forecasting, and scenario simulation.

3. Float

Float is a cash flow forecasting software specifically designed for small businesses. It offers real-time tracking, budgeting, and scenario planning features, making it a comprehensive solution for managing cash flow.

4. PlanGuru

PlanGuru is a powerful financial planning and forecasting software that offers cash flow forecasting capabilities. It allows businesses to create detailed cash flow projections by integrating with their accounting systems.

Integrating Forecasting with Accounting Systems

Integrating cash flow forecasting with accounting systems can greatly improve forecasting accuracy and efficiency. With the ability to access financial data in real-time, businesses can quickly make adjustments to their cash flow forecasts based on actual results. Integrating forecasting with accounting systems also allows for more transparency and collaboration within an organization. Different departments can have access to the same data, leading to better decision-making and a more cohesive approach to managing cash flow. There are several ways businesses can integrate cash flow forecasting with their accounting systems. Some software offers seamless integration, while others may require additional customization or use of third-party tools. It is important for businesses to choose software and systems that can easily integrate with each other for a smooth and efficient forecasting process.

In conclusion, utilizing technology for cash flow forecasting is essential for businesses to effectively manage their cash flow and make informed decisions. With the right software and integration strategies, businesses can improve forecasting accuracy, save time, and adapt to changing market conditions with ease. As technology continues to evolve, it is only expected that the benefits of utilizing it for cash flow forecasting will continue to grow.

Chapter 12: Common Cash Flow Ratios – Interpreting and Using Ratios to Identify Issues and Improve Cash Flow

Cash flow is at the heart of every business, and it is essential to have a clear understanding of your cash flow situation to make informed decisions and plan for the future. One way to gain a better understanding of your cash flow is by using ratios. These ratios can help you identify potential issues and improve your cash flow management. In this chapter, we will explore some common cash flow ratios and how to interpret and use them to improve cash flow.

Common Cash Flow Ratios

Before we dive into interpreting and using ratios, it is essential to have a basic understanding of the most common cash flow ratios. Here are five ratios that every business owner should be familiar with:

1. Operating Cash Flow Ratio

This ratio measures a company's ability to generate cash from its operations, which is essential for the day-to-day operations and expenses of the business. A higher operating cash flow ratio indicates that a company has sufficient cash flow to cover its operating expenses. A lower ratio may indicate that a company is struggling to generate enough cash flow to sustain its operations.

2. Cash Ratio

The cash ratio reflects a company's ability to cover its short-term obligations with its current cash reserves. A high cash ratio indicates that a company is in a good position to meet its short-term financial obligations, while a low cash ratio may indicate that a company may struggle to pay its bills on time.

3. Cash Conversion Cycle

The cash conversion cycle measures the time it takes for a business to convert its inventory into cash. It is calculated by subtracting the number of days it takes to pay suppliers from the number of days it takes to collect payments from customers. A shorter cash conversion cycle is typically better, as it means that a company can quickly turn its inventory into cash.

4. Debt-to-Cash Ratio

This ratio compares a company's total debt to its total cash reserve. A high debt-to-cash ratio may indicate that a company is carrying too much debt, and this could impact its ability to generate cash flow in the future.

5. Debt-to-Equity Ratio

Similar to the debt-to-cash ratio, the debt-to-equity ratio measures a company's level of debt compared to its equity. A high ratio may indicate that a company is relying heavily on debt to fund its operations, which could be a red flag for potential cash flow issues.

Now that we have discussed some common cash flow ratios, let's explore how to interpret and use them to identify issues and improve cash flow.

Interpreting and Using Ratios to Identify Issues

Ratios are only useful if you understand what they mean and know how to use them to your advantage. Here are some tips on interpreting ratios and using them to identify potential issues with your cash flow:

Compare Ratios to Industry Averages

One way to interpret ratios is by comparing them to industry averages. While every industry is different, having an idea of what is considered a healthy ratio in your industry can give you a benchmark to strive for. If your ratios fall significantly below industry averages, it may be a sign that you need to reassess your cash flow management.

Look for Trends

It's essential to track your ratios over time and look for any patterns or trends. For example, if you notice that your operating cash flow ratio has been steadily declining over the past few months, it could be a sign of a larger issue with your cash flow management.

Consider Your Company's Lifecycle

Different stages of a company's lifecycle may impact its cash flow ratios. For example, a startup may have a lower debt-to-cash ratio because it is investing heavily in growth, while a mature company may have a higher ratio as it pays off its debt. It's essential to consider the stage of your company when interpreting ratios.

Using Ratios to Improve Cash Flow

Now that we understand how to interpret ratios let's explore how to use them to improve cash flow. Here are some practical tips on how to use ratios to your advantage:

Identify Areas for Improvement

Ratios can help you identify where your cash flow may be struggling. For example, if your cash conversion cycle is longer than industry averages, it may be a sign that you need to work on improving your inventory management to generate cash faster.

Set Goals and Track Progress

Once you have identified areas for improvement, use ratios to set goals and track your progress. For example, if your debt-to-cash ratio is high, set a goal to pay off a certain amount of debt each month to bring the ratio down. Tracking your progress will help you stay focused and motivated.

Make Informed Decisions

Ratios can also help you make more informed decisions when it comes to managing your cash flow. For example, if you are considering taking on more debt, you can reference your debt-to-equity ratio to determine if you have enough cash reserves to support the increased debt. Additionally, comparing ratios to industry averages can help guide your decision-making.

Regularly Monitor Ratios

Lastly, it's essential to monitor your ratios regularly to stay on top of any changes and address potential issues before they become significant problems. By keeping a close eye on your ratios, you can make proactive adjustments to improve your cash flow.

In conclusion, understanding and using ratios can be a powerful tool in managing your cash flow. By regularly tracking and interpreting ratios, you can identify potential issues and make informed decisions to improve your cash flow. Remember to compare ratios to industry averages, track trends, and consider the stage of your company when interpreting ratios. Use ratios to set goals, make informed decisions, and regularly monitor your progress. With these tips, you can improve your cash flow management and set your business up for success.

Chapter 13: Scenario Planning for Cash Flow Forecasting

Why Scenario Planning is Important

In today's fast-paced, ever-changing business landscape, the ability to plan for unexpected events and potential risks is crucial for success. This is where scenario planning comes in. It is a strategic management tool that allows businesses to prepare for a range of possible outcomes and make informed decisions based on those scenarios. In the context of cash flow forecasting, scenario planning helps businesses to identify potential cash flow disruptions and implement strategies to mitigate their impact. One of the main reasons why scenario planning is important for cash flow forecasting is that it allows businesses to be prepared for unexpected events. As we have seen in recent years, unexpected events such as natural disasters, economic downturns, and global pandemics can have a significant impact on a business' cash flow. By creating different scenarios, businesses can identify potential risks and develop strategies to minimize their impact on cash flow.

In addition, scenario planning also helps businesses to have a better understanding of their financial health. By creating scenarios that reflect different market conditions and operational challenges, businesses can get a realistic view of their financial situation and make more informed decisions. This is especially important for small businesses with limited resources, as cash flow disruptions can have a severe impact on their operations.

Creating Different Scenarios

To create effective scenarios for cash flow forecasting, businesses need to consider various factors that can affect their cash flow. This includes external factors, such as changes in the market, industry trends, and economic conditions, as well as internal factors, such as sales projections, operational costs, and payment terms. By assessing these factors, businesses can develop a range of scenarios that reflect different outcomes. The first step in creating scenarios is identifying potential risks and uncertainties that can affect cash flow. This could include a sudden decrease in sales, increase in operational costs, delayed payments from clients, or changes in market conditions. Once these risks are identified, businesses can then create different scenarios based on the severity of the risk and its potential impact on cash flow.

Creating scenarios also requires businesses to analyze historical data and trends. By looking at past data, businesses can identify patterns and make projections for the future. This can help in creating more accurate and realistic scenarios. It is also important to involve key stakeholders in the scenario planning process, as their insights and perspectives can add value and identify potential blind spots.

Adjusting Strategies Based on Scenarios

The purpose of scenario planning is not just to identify potential risks, but also to develop strategies to mitigate their impact and safeguard cash flow. Once different scenarios have been created, businesses need to analyze each one and identify the best course of action for each scenario. This could involve changing payment terms, reducing operational costs, renegotiating contracts, or seeking additional funding. The key to effectively managing cash flow through scenario planning is flexibility. Businesses need to be prepared to adjust their strategies depending on the scenario that unfolds. For example, if sales projections are not met, businesses may need to implement cost-cutting measures to maintain a positive cash flow. Conversely, if sales exceed projections, businesses can use the cash surplus to invest in growth opportunities. Furthermore, businesses need to regularly revisit and update their scenarios to adapt to changing market conditions and internal factors. This will help businesses to stay proactive and adjust strategies accordingly, rather than being reactive to unexpected events.

In conclusion, scenario planning is a vital tool for cash flow forecasting. By creating different scenarios and adjusting strategies based on those scenarios, businesses can better prepare for potential risks and manage their cash flow more effectively. In today's uncertain business landscape, this is an essential practice for any business looking to maintain financial stability and achieve long-term success.

Chapter 14: Managing Cash Flow During Growth

Challenges for Growing Businesses

Congratulations! Your business has successfully grown and is thriving. However, with growth comes new challenges, and one of the most critical challenges for businesses is managing cash flow. As your business expands, so too do your expenses, and it may become more challenging to keep track of all your incoming and outgoing cash. In addition, you may also face delays in payment from clients or suppliers, which can create significant cash flow gaps. In the excitement of growth, it's crucial to not overlook the importance of managing your cash flow. Failure to do so can result in a cash crunch, even for businesses that are experiencing success. In fact, poor cash flow management is one of the main reasons that many small businesses fail. Therefore, it's crucial to have a solid plan in place to handle cash flow during growth.

Strategies for Handling Cash Flow During Growth

1. Create a Cash Flow Forecast: One of the best ways to handle cash flow during growth is to have a clear picture of your cash flow. A cash flow forecast helps you anticipate any potential cash flow issues and allows you to plan accordingly. With an accurate forecast, you can prepare for any upcoming expenses or delays in payment, ensuring that you have enough cash on hand to keep your business running smoothly.

2. Monitor Your Receivables: As your business grows, you may be dealing with a larger number of clients or customers. It's essential to track your accounts receivable carefully and follow up with any late payments. Consider implementing a system to incentivize early payments or penalties for late payments to encourage timely payments and improve your cash flow.

3. Control Expenses: As your business expands, so too do your expenses. It's crucial to keep a close eye on your expenses and identify any areas where you can cut costs. For example, look for more cost-effective suppliers or negotiate better deals with current

vendors. By keeping your expenses in check, you'll have more cash on hand to invest in your business' growth or handle any unexpected cash flow gaps.

4. Increase Sales: Growth often means an increase in sales, but it's important to be strategic in your sales initiatives. Instead of focusing solely on increasing revenue, consider which products or services have the highest profit margins and focus your efforts there. This approach will allow you to generate more cash for your business without straining your cash flow.

5. Source Additional Financing: In times of growth, you may require additional funding to cover expansion costs or cash flow gaps. It's crucial to plan ahead and explore financing options before you run into a cash flow crunch. Options include bank loans, lines of credit, or even seeking investments from outside sources. Just be sure to assess the terms and risks carefully and have a plan in place to repay any borrowed funds.

Importance of Long-Term Planning

When it comes to managing cash flow during growth, taking a long-term approach is vital. It's essential to have a strategic plan in place for managing your cash flow not just for the next few months, but for the next few years. As your business continues to grow, your cash flow will become more complex, and having a clear long-term plan can help you make informed decisions and stay on track. Take the time to regularly review and adjust your cash flow forecast, keeping in mind your business growth goals and any potential roadblocks. By staying proactive and planning ahead, you'll be better equipped to handle any cash flow challenges that may come your way during periods of growth.

In conclusion, managing cash flow during growth is a crucial aspect of business success. By creating a cash flow forecast, monitoring your receivables, controlling expenses, increasing sales, and having a long-term plan in place, you'll be able to navigate the challenges of growth and ensure that your business continues to thrive. Stay proactive, be strategic, and never lose sight of the importance of managing your cash flow.

Chapter 15: Cash Flow Forecasting During Economic Downturns

During challenging economic times, businesses of all sizes are faced with the reality of limited resources and a decrease in revenue. As a result, maintaining a positive cash flow becomes crucial for survival and growth. In this chapter, we will explore key considerations during economic downturns, strategies for maintaining positive cash flow, and how to prepare for economic uncertainty.

Key Considerations During Downturns

The saying "hope for the best, but prepare for the worst" holds true when it comes to managing cash flow during an economic downturn. It is important to anticipate potential challenges and have a plan in place to mitigate their impact. Some key considerations include:

Assessing Risks and Creating Contingency Plans

The first step in preparing for a potential economic downturn is to assess the risks to your business. This could include analyzing factors such as changes in consumer behavior, shifts in the market, and potential disruptions to your supply chain. Once risks have been identified, creating contingency plans can help mitigate their impact and ensure continuity of operations.

Reviewing and Adjusting Budgets

During economic downturns, it is important to review and adjust your budgets accordingly. This may involve cutting expenses, reducing inventory levels, and prioritizing spending on essential items. By closely monitoring your budget, you can make informed decisions and avoid overspending.

Strengthening Relationships with Vendors and Creditors

Maintaining positive relationships with vendors and creditors is crucial during times of economic uncertainty. Stay in communication with them and work together to find mutually beneficial solutions, such as renegotiating payment terms or finding alternative sources of financing.

Keeping a Buffer of Cash Reserves

Having a buffer of cash reserves can be a lifesaver during an economic downturn. This can provide a financial cushion to cover unexpected expenses and allow your business to continue operating smoothly.

Strategies for Maintaining Positive Cash Flow

Maintaining positive cash flow is essential for businesses in good times and bad. During an economic downturn, implementing these strategies can help your business stay afloat and even thrive:

Accelerating Inflows

To maintain positive cash flow, businesses should look for ways to accelerate their inflows. One way to achieve this is by offering discounts or promotions for early payments from customers. Additionally, businesses can explore alternative methods of payment, such as accepting credit card payments or setting up recurring billing.

Delaying Outflows

Delaying outflows is another powerful strategy for maintaining positive cash flow. This can be achieved by negotiating extended payment terms with vendors and suppliers or by delaying non-essential expenses until the economic situation improves.

Staying on Top of Invoicing and Collections

During an economic downturn, it is even more crucial to stay on top of invoicing and collections. Be diligent in sending out invoices on time and follow up with customers who are past due on payments. Consider offering flexible payment options to help customers who may also be struggling during these difficult times.

Investing in Quality Over Quantity

With limited resources, it's important to make smart investments that will yield long-term benefits. This means focusing on quality over quantity when it comes to purchases and investments. Consider investing in tools or technology that can increase efficiency and reduce costs in the long run.

Preparing for Economic Uncertainty

While it may be impossible to predict the future, businesses can take steps to prepare for economic uncertainty. Some strategies to consider include:

Building a Cash Flow Forecast

Having a cash flow forecast can help businesses anticipate future cash flow needs and prepare for potential challenges. It allows businesses to identify potential cash flow gaps and plan accordingly.

Diversifying Revenue Streams

Relying on a single source of revenue can leave businesses vulnerable during an economic downturn. Diversifying revenue streams can help mitigate this risk by providing alternative sources of income. This could include expanding into new markets or offering new products or services.

Investing in Marketing

While it may seem counterintuitive to invest in marketing during a downturn, it can be a smart move. Promoting your business and staying relevant in the minds of consumers can help you maintain a steady stream of cash flow.

Upskilling and Cross-Training Employees

During an economic downturn, businesses may be forced to cut back on staffing. By investing in upskilling and cross-training employees, businesses can ensure that they have a versatile and competent team that can handle different roles and responsibilities as needed.

In conclusion, preparing for economic downturns and implementing strategies to maintain positive cash flow are crucial for the long-term success of any business. By being proactive and adaptable, businesses can not only survive but also thrive during challenging economic times.

Chapter 16: Cash Flow Forecasting for Different Types of Businesses

Cash Flow Forecasting for Service-Based Businesses

Cash flow forecasting is a critical tool for service-based businesses, as it allows them to plan ahead and identify potential cash shortages or surpluses. In the service industry, cash flow fluctuations can occur due to a variety of factors, such as seasonality, unexpected expenses, or changes in client demand. Therefore, having a clear understanding of your business's cash inflows and outflows is crucial for maintaining stability and sustaining growth. One of the key strategies for cash flow forecasting in service-based businesses is to accurately estimate the timing of your cash inflows. Service businesses often have a longer billing cycle, with invoices sometimes taking weeks or even months to be paid. Therefore, it is essential to track your invoicing and payment processes carefully. You can also consider offering discounts for upfront payments or implementing a pre-payment policy to improve your cash flow. Another important consideration for service-based businesses is managing your expenses. Keep a close eye on your operating costs and find ways to reduce unnecessary expenses. For example, you can negotiate better deals with vendors or review your subscription services to eliminate unnecessary fees. This will help you maintain a healthy cash flow and allocate funds for future investments.

Cash Flow Forecasting for Retail Businesses

For retail businesses, cash flow forecasting is crucial to managing inventory and avoiding stock shortages and overstocking. With the rise of e-commerce, retail businesses also need to consider the timing and costs of shipping and handling, as these can significantly impact cash flow. Predicting consumer demand and staying on top of inventory turnover rates is essential for successful cash flow management in the retail industry. An effective cash flow management strategy for retail businesses is to closely monitor sales trends and adjust your inventory levels accordingly. Consider using software or tools to analyze sales data and identify trends and patterns that can help you make more accurate sales forecasts. Additionally, implementing a cash flow budget can help you set goals and make informed decisions about future investments.

In the retail industry, seasonal fluctuations can heavily impact cash flow. Depending on the type of products or services your business offers, you may experience a surge in sales during specific times of the year. Use historical data and market trends to anticipate these changes and plan for them in your cash flow forecast. This will help you avoid cash flow shortages and prepare for increased sales during busy seasons.

Cash Flow Forecasting for Manufacturing Businesses

In the manufacturing industry, cash flow forecasting is crucial for managing production and inventory costs. Manufacturing businesses often have high overhead costs, with expenses such as raw materials, labor, and machinery. Tracking and managing these expenses is essential for maintaining a healthy cash flow. One strategy for cash flow forecasting in manufacturing businesses is to conduct a break-even analysis. This will help you determine the minimum amount of sales needed to cover your production costs and achieve profitability. Use this information to make informed decisions about pricing, production volume, and inventory levels.

For manufacturing businesses, supply chain management is also a critical factor in cash flow forecasting. Delays or disruptions in the supply chain can significantly impact your business's cash flow. Therefore, it is essential to maintain strong relationships with your suppliers and have backup plans in place in case of any issues.

Closing Thoughts

In conclusion, cash flow forecasting is an essential practice for businesses of all types and sizes. By accurately predicting your business's cash inflows and outflows, you can make informed decisions about expenses, investments, and overall financial planning. The key to successful cash flow forecasting is to regularly review and update your forecasts, use historical data and market trends for guidance, and be proactive in managing your cash flow. With these strategies in place, your business can maintain a healthy cash flow and achieve long-term success.

Chapter 17: Cash Flow Forecasting for Seasonal Businesses

Challenges for Seasonal Businesses

Seasonal businesses face unique challenges when it comes to managing their cash flow. Their business income and expenses can vary greatly throughout the year, making it difficult to predict and plan for cash flow fluctuations. For example, a business that operates a ski resort may see high revenue during the winter months but very little during the off-season. This can create cash flow gaps and cause stress for business owners and their financial management team.

Another challenge for seasonal businesses is the need to balance cash flow during peak and off-peak periods. During peak periods, there may be a surge in demand for products or services, which requires an increase in inventory or staffing. This can lead to higher cash outflows, which need to be carefully managed to ensure they do not exceed the incoming cash flow. On the other hand, during slow periods, businesses may struggle to cover their fixed expenses such as rent and utilities.

Strategies for Managing Fluctuations and Maintaining Cash Flow

Despite these challenges, there are strategies that seasonal businesses can use to effectively manage fluctuations and maintain a positive cash flow. Here are a few tips to consider:

1. Create a detailed cash flow forecast

The first step in managing cash flow for a seasonal business is to create a cash flow forecast for the entire year. This should include both peak and off-peak periods, as well as any expected expenses and income. Use historical data to estimate the timing and amount of cash inflows and outflows. This will help identify potential cash flow gaps and allow you to plan accordingly.

2. Cut unnecessary expenses

During slow periods, it is important to reduce expenses to help maintain a positive cash flow. This may mean cutting back on non-essential expenses such as marketing, travel, or inventory purchases. Review your budget and identify areas where you can make cuts without negatively impacting the business.

3. Prepare for slow periods

Take advantage of the busy season to build up a cash reserve that can be used during slow periods. This will help you cover fixed expenses and keep your business running smoothly. It may also be beneficial to negotiate payment terms with suppliers, allowing for more flexibility in cash outflows during the slower months.

4. Improve cash flow timing

Consider offering discounts to customers who pay early or implementing a late payment penalty to encourage timely payments from clients. This can help improve the timing of cash inflows, making it easier to manage expenses during slow periods. You may also want to consider adjusting your billing cycle to align with your peak season, allowing for more consistent cash flow throughout the year.

5. Diversify your product or service offerings

If possible, consider expanding your product or service offerings to attract customers during your off-season. This can help generate additional revenue and mitigate the impact of slow periods on your cash flow. It may also be beneficial to explore different target markets or geographical locations to lessen the impact of seasonal fluctuations.

6. Utilize technology

Technology can play a crucial role in helping seasonal businesses better manage their cash flow. There are various cash flow forecasting tools and software available that can provide real-time insights to help identify potential issues and make more informed financial decisions. You may also want to consider online payment methods to streamline the collection of payments from customers.

In conclusion, managing cash flow for seasonal businesses can be a daunting task, but it is not impossible. By creating a detailed cash flow forecast, cutting unnecessary expenses, planning for slow periods, improving cash flow timing, diversifying offerings, and utilizing technology, businesses can better manage fluctuations and maintain a positive cash flow throughout the year. With careful planning and strategic implementation, seasonal businesses can thrive even in the face of seasonal challenges.

Chapter 18: Cash Flow Forecasting for Small Businesses

Cash flow forecasting is an essential tool for all businesses, no matter their size. However, when it comes to small businesses, there are unique considerations that must be taken into account. As a small business owner, you are not only responsible for the day-to-day operations of your company, but also for its long-term success and growth. This is where effective cash flow forecasting becomes crucial.

Unique Considerations for Small Businesses

Small businesses often have limited resources and a closer connection to their finances compared to larger corporations. As a result, cash flow forecasting for small businesses requires a more hands-on and detailed approach. Here are some unique considerations to keep in mind when creating your cash flow forecast.

1. Seasonal Fluctuations:
Many small businesses experience seasonal fluctuations in their revenue and cash flow. For example, a retail business may see a surge in sales during the holiday season, while a landscaping company may have lower income during the winter months. It is important to anticipate these fluctuations in your forecast to avoid cash flow shortages during slower periods.

2. Dependence on Key Clients:
Small businesses often rely on a few key clients for the majority of their revenue. If one of these clients experiences financial difficulties or cuts back on their spending, it could significantly impact the cash flow of your business. It is essential to diversify your client base and not become too dependent on a few customers.

3. Limited Credit Options:
Unlike large corporations, small businesses may not have access to large lines of credit or other financing options. This means that cash flow shortages can have a more significant impact and may require more creative solutions. It is crucial to monitor your cash flow closely and plan for any potential shortages well in advance.

Planning for Growth

As a small business owner, your ultimate goal is to grow and expand your company. However, growth comes with its own set of challenges, including managing cash flow effectively. Here are some strategies for incorporating growth into your cash flow forecasting.

1. Future Expenses:
When creating a cash flow forecast, it is important to consider not only your current expenses but also any future expenses that may arise due to growth. This could include hiring additional staff, purchasing new equipment, or expanding your physical space. By incorporating these expenses into your forecast, you can better plan for them and avoid cash flow issues.

2. Customer Retention:
While attracting new customers is essential for growth, don't overlook the importance of retaining your existing customers. A loyal customer base can provide steady and predictable income, which is crucial for managing cash flow. Consider implementing customer retention strategies when forecasting for growth.

3. Contingency Planning:
As mentioned earlier, small businesses often have limited access to credit options. In the event of unexpected expenses or cash flow shortages, it is essential to have contingency plans in place. This could include negotiating payment terms with suppliers, offering promotions to increase sales, or seeking alternative funding sources.

Managing Cash Flow with Limited Resources

With limited resources, small businesses must be strategic in how they manage their cash flow. Here are some tips to help you make the most of your resources and maintain a healthy cash flow.

1. Streamline Processes:
Inefficient processes can eat into your cash flow and eat up valuable time that could be used for other tasks. As a small business, it is crucial to regularly assess your

processes and streamline wherever possible. This could mean automating tasks, outsourcing non-essential tasks, or negotiating better deals with suppliers.

2. Cash Flow Surpluses:

While cash flow shortages are a top concern for small businesses, it is also essential to plan for cash flow surpluses. This could happen if your sales exceed expectations or if you receive early payments from customers. By preparing for surpluses in your forecast, you can use the extra cash strategically, such as paying off debt or making investments for future growth.

3. Be Realistic:

When it comes to cash flow forecasting, it is crucial to be realistic in your projections. While it's essential to have ambitious goals for your small business, your cash flow forecast should reflect your current situation and expected growth. Overestimating sales or underestimating expenses can lead to unrealistic expectations and cash flow issues in the future.

In conclusion, small businesses have unique considerations when it comes to cash flow forecasting. By taking these considerations into account and creating a comprehensive forecast that plans for both growth and potential challenges, you can ensure the financial success of your small business. Remember to regularly review and adjust your forecasts as your business grows and evolves, and seek the help of a financial advisor for additional support and guidance. With proper cash flow management, your small business can thrive and achieve its full potential.

Chapter 19: Cash Flow Forecasting for Large Corporations

In the fast-paced and ever-changing world of business, large corporations face unique challenges when it comes to cash flow forecasting. With higher revenues, more complex operations, and larger budgets, these companies require sophisticated and robust strategies for successful cash flow management. In this chapter, we will explore the complexities of cash flow forecasting for large corporations and discuss strategies for handling large amounts of data and risk management.

Complexities of Cash Flow Forecasting for Large Corporations

As a large corporation, your cash flow can be affected by a multitude of factors such as seasonality, economic conditions, and industry trends. With multiple departments, subsidiaries, and international operations, the sheer volume of data to be analyzed and managed can be overwhelming. It is crucial for corporations to have a deep understanding of their cash inflows and outflows in order to make informed financial decisions. Furthermore, large corporations often have more diversified revenue streams, making it difficult to accurately forecast cash flow. This complexity can also be compounded by varying payment schedules and collection processes from different clients. All of these factors make cash flow forecasting for large corporations more challenging and require a comprehensive approach to ensure financial stability.

Strategies for Handling Large Amounts of Data

In order to effectively forecast cash flow, large corporations need to have a strong grasp on their financial data. This means collecting and organizing data from various sources such as sales records, billing statements, and accounts payable and receivable. It is vital for corporations to have a system in place for managing and updating this data regularly. To handle the high volume of data, large corporations can utilize technology and data analysis tools to streamline the forecasting process. These tools can help in identifying trends and patterns in cash flow data, making it easier to project future cash flows. Additionally, automating processes such as invoicing and billing can help reduce errors and improve cash flow management.

Another effective strategy for handling large amounts of data is to centralize financial data in one location. This can be accomplished through the implementation of an Enterprise Resource Planning (ERP) system. By consolidating financial data in one platform, large corporations can have a real-time view of their cash flow and make more accurate forecasts.

Risk Management

Risk management is a crucial aspect of cash flow forecasting for large corporations. With higher revenues and more diversified operations, corporations are exposed to a wider range of risks such as economic downturns, market volatility, and changes in regulations. These risks can have a significant impact on cash flow, and it is essential for corporations to analyze and mitigate these risks. One strategy for risk management in cash flow forecasting is scenario planning. By creating multiple scenarios, corporations can assess the potential impact of different risks on their cash flow. This allows for more informed decision-making in times of uncertainty. Large corporations should also consider implementing hedging strategies to mitigate risks associated with foreign currency exchange. This can help reduce the impact of currency fluctuations on cash flow and provide stability in international operations. In addition, large corporations should regularly review and adjust their cash flow forecasting strategies to adapt to changing circumstances. This may include reevaluating budgeting processes, revisiting sales forecasts, and staying abreast of industry trends. By continuously monitoring and adjusting their strategies, corporations can better manage risk and maintain stable cash flow.

In conclusion, cash flow forecasting for large corporations requires a tailored and comprehensive approach due to the complexities of operations and high volume of data. By understanding these challenges and adopting effective strategies for managing data and risk, corporations can make more accurate forecasts and ensure financial stability in the long run.

Chapter 20: Cash Flow Forecasting for Nonprofit Organizations

Unique Challenges for Nonprofits

Nonprofit organizations face a unique set of challenges when it comes to managing cash flow. Unlike for-profit businesses, nonprofits rely heavily on donations and grants for income, making their revenue streams less predictable. In addition, budget constraints often result in limited resources and the need to carefully manage expenses. This can create a delicate balancing act between maintaining adequate cash flow and fulfilling the organization's mission. One of the main challenges for nonprofits is managing cash flow during seasonal or fluctuating periods of giving. For example, many nonprofits see an increase in donations at the end of the calendar year as people look for tax deductions. This can lead to a cash flow surplus in the short term, but without proper planning, it can quickly turn into a deficit in the following months.

Another challenge for nonprofits is managing restricted funds. Donors often specify how their contributions should be used, which can limit the organization's flexibility in allocating funds to cover expenses. This can also create cash flow constraints if the organization relies heavily on restricted funds for its operations.

Strategies for Maintaining Stable Cash Flow ·

Despite these challenges, there are several strategies that nonprofits can implement to maintain stable cash flow and ensure the organization's financial health. The first step is to develop a comprehensive cash flow forecast that takes into account all sources of income and expenses. This should include not only donations and grants but also other sources such as membership fees, event revenues, and investment income. By projecting cash flow for at least the next 12 months, nonprofits can better anticipate potential fluctuations and plan accordingly. Another strategy is to diversify revenue streams. While donations and grants may be the main sources of income for many nonprofits, it's important to explore other sources of revenue. This can include fundraising events, product sales, or fee-based services that align with the organization's mission. By increasing revenue diversification, nonprofits can reduce their reliance on a single income source and create a more stable cash flow. Nonprofits should also regularly review and adjust their budget to ensure it aligns with their goals and financial reality. This can involve identifying areas of unnecessary spending and reallocating funds to more critical areas. By regularly tracking and analyzing cash flow, nonprofits can make informed decisions and adjust as needed to maintain a stable financial position.

Importance of Donor Management

Donors are a vital part of nonprofit organizations, and maintaining strong relationships with donors is crucial for maintaining a stable cash flow. This involves not only thanking donors for their contributions but also keeping them informed about the organization's achievements and the impact of their donations. Nonprofits should also make an effort to diversify their donor base, rather than relying on a small group of donors for the majority of their funding. This not only reduces risk but also opens up potential sources of funding from different individuals and organizations. Effective donor management also involves regular communication and transparency. Nonprofits should share their financial status with donors and keep them informed of any major changes or challenges. By building trust and open communication with donors, nonprofits can maintain a steady flow of contributions and support for their mission.

In conclusion, cash flow forecasting is critical for the financial stability of nonprofit organizations. By understanding the unique challenges they face, implementing strategies for maintaining stable cash flow, and prioritizing donor management, nonprofits can ensure their financial health and continue to fulfill their mission for years to come.

Chapter 21: Cash Flow Forecasting in International Business

Factors to Consider for International Cash Flow

When it comes to cash flow forecasting in international business, there are a number of factors that must be taken into consideration. These include political and economic stability, cultural differences, legal and tax regulations, and exchange rates. Each of these can have a significant impact on a company's cash flow both in the short and long term.

In order to ensure the accuracy and success of your international cash flow forecasting, it is important to thoroughly research and analyze these factors for each country or region that your business operates in. This will help you identify potential risks and fluctuations, and make informed decisions for your forecast.

Managing Currency Fluctuations

One of the biggest challenges of international cash flow forecasting is managing currency fluctuations. These fluctuations can greatly affect the value of your company's assets and liabilities, as well as its overall cash flow. In order to mitigate this risk, it is important to have a solid currency risk management strategy in place.

This can include using hedging techniques such as forward contracts or options to protect against currency fluctuations. It is also crucial to closely monitor and analyze currency trends and make adjustments to your forecast as needed. Additionally, partnering with banks or financial institutions that specialize in international business can provide valuable insights and assistance in managing currency fluctuations.

Strategies for Successful International Cash Flow Forecasting

In order to achieve successful international cash flow forecasting, there are a number of strategies that businesses can implement. First and foremost, it is important to establish a reliable and accurate cash flow forecasting system. This can include implementing a cloud-based software that can easily track and analyze cash flow across multiple currencies and locations. Additionally, businesses should regularly review and update their forecast to reflect any changes in economic and political conditions. This can help anticipate potential cash flow gaps or surpluses and make necessary adjustments. Another key strategy is to maintain strong relationships with international partners and suppliers. Building trust and open communication can help alleviate any potential cash flow issues and foster long-term partnerships. Moreover, utilizing scenario planning can be beneficial in creating contingency plans for potential cash flow disruptions. This can help mitigate risks and ensure the company has enough liquidity to handle unexpected events. Lastly, it is important to continuously monitor and analyze the company's international cash flow performance. This can help identify any areas for improvement and make necessary adjustments to the forecasting process.

In conclusion, successful cash flow forecasting in international business requires a thorough understanding of various factors such as political and economic stability, currency fluctuations, and cultural differences. By implementing effective strategies, businesses can mitigate risks and ensure accurate and reliable cash flow forecasting.

Chapter 22: Cash Flow Forecasting for Startups

Starting a new business can be an exhilarating and challenging experience. As a startup, you are faced with a unique set of challenges, from securing funding to building your brand and attracting customers. With so much to focus on, it's easy to overlook the importance of cash flow forecasting. However, for startups, cash flow forecasting is crucial for ensuring financial stability and long-term success.

Unique Challenges for Startups

As a startup, you are in the early stages of your business journey. You may not have established a stable customer base or have a steady stream of income. Therefore, cash flow can be unpredictable and often tight. With limited resources, every expense must be carefully considered and managed.

Additionally, startups may face difficulties in securing funding. Without a proven track record or assets to offer as collateral, it can be challenging to obtain loans or investment. This lack of financial stability can make cash flow management even more critical for the survival of your startup.

Strategies for Managing Cash Flow During Early Stages

The key to successfully managing cash flow during the early stages of a startup is to be proactive and strategic. Here are some strategies to consider:

1. Accurate Cash Flow Forecasting

The first step in managing cash flow is to have an accurate understanding of your current and projected cash flows. This will help you identify potential cash flow issues before they arise and allow you to make informed decisions about your spending.

2. Prepare for Unexpected Expenses

In the early stages of a startup, unexpected expenses can occur frequently. It's essential to plan for these with a buffer in your cash flow forecast. This can prevent any major setbacks in case of unexpected costs.

3. Negotiate Terms with Vendors

When starting a business, cash on hand is limited. It's essential to negotiate payment terms with vendors that align with your cash flow. This can help you manage your cash flow effectively and avoid any immediate cash shortages.

4. Focus on Cash Flow Before Profit

In the early stages of a startup, it's crucial to prioritize cash flow over profits. Keep a close eye on your cash flow forecast and make adjustments to ensure you have enough cash to keep your business running. Profits will come in time once your business is stable.

Long-Term Planning

While it's vital to manage cash flow in the early stages of a startup, it's also crucial to have a long-term plan in place. Here are some steps to consider for long-term cash flow planning:

1. Set Realistic Goals

Having clear and achievable goals for your startup can help you stay focused and make the necessary financial decisions to achieve those goals. Outline your objectives and break them down into smaller, achievable targets. This can help you monitor your progress and make adjustments as needed to meet your goals.

2. Monitor Cash Flow Performance

As your startup grows, it's crucial to monitor your cash flow performance continuously. Compare your actual cash flow to your forecasted cash flow to identify any discrepancies and make necessary changes. This can help you stay on top of your finances and make informed decisions for your business.

3. Seek Professional Help

Managing cash flow effectively can be a challenge for startups, especially if you have limited experience in financial management. Consider seeking help from a professional financial advisor who can provide guidance and support in forecasting and managing your cash flow.

4. Don't Neglect Sales and Marketing

Finally, don't neglect sales and marketing efforts for your startup. A steady stream of income is vital for maintaining a healthy cash flow. Invest time and resources into promoting your brand, attracting new customers, and retaining existing ones.

Taking a proactive and strategic approach to cash flow forecasting and management can greatly benefit startups in the long run. By understanding your unique challenges and implementing the right strategies, you can ensure the financial stability and success of your business.

Chapter 23: Communicating Cash Flow Forecasts to Stakeholders

Cash flow forecasting is an essential tool for businesses of all sizes. It allows companies to analyze their future financial position and make informed decisions based on that information. However, the value of cash flow forecasting is only maximized when it is effectively communicated to stakeholders. In this chapter, we will explore the importance of effectively communicating cash flow forecasts and provide tips on how to do so in a way that is clear, transparent, and useful.

Communicating Cash Flow Forecasts to Stakeholders

Stakeholders are individuals or groups with a vested interest in a company's financial performance. This could include investors, creditors, employees, customers, and even the general public. As a business owner or financial manager, it's essential to keep stakeholders informed about the company's financial health and future projections. This is where cash flow forecasting comes into play. Communicating cash flow forecasts to stakeholders is crucial because it allows them to have a clear understanding of the company's financial state. By sharing forecasts, you are demonstrating transparency and building trust with stakeholders. This can help strengthen relationships and improve transparency, thereby enhancing the company's reputation. When communicating with stakeholders, it's important to keep the language simple and avoid using technical jargon. Remember, not everyone may have the same level of financial knowledge, so it's vital to make the information understandable for everyone. Consider preparing multiple versions of your cash flow forecast – a detailed version for internal use and a simplified version for external stakeholders.

Using Forecasts to Make Informed Decisions

Cash flow forecasts aren't just essential for stakeholders – they also play a crucial role in decision-making for businesses. By having a clear understanding of projected cash flow, businesses can make informed decisions about investments, hiring, pricing, and other critical financial aspects. For example, if a forecast shows a potential cash flow shortfall in the future, the company can take proactive measures to address the issue, such as cutting costs or securing additional financing. On the other hand, if a forecast shows an excess of cash flow, the business can make decisions about how to best utilize those funds, such as investing in growth opportunities or returning capital to shareholders.

By utilizing cash flow forecasts, businesses can avoid making impulsive decisions and instead make strategic, data-driven choices that align with their long-term goals. Communicating these forecasts to stakeholders enables everyone to be on the same page and work together towards the company's success.

Maintaining Transparency

Transparency is a crucial factor in building trust with stakeholders. When it comes to cash flow forecasting, it's essential to be transparent about the assumptions and methodology used in creating the forecast. This means being clear about sources of data, the timeline for accuracy of projections, and any external factors that could impact cash flow. Maintaining transparency also involves regularly updating stakeholders on changes to the forecast. As business conditions can change quickly, it's important to keep stakeholders informed in a timely manner. This demonstrates that the company is actively managing its finances and is committed to staying on top of any changes that may impact cash flow. Another way to maintain transparency is by providing access to the cash flow forecast to stakeholders. This could be in the form of a shared document or a dashboard that allows stakeholders to monitor the forecast in real-time. By providing this level of access, stakeholders can see the forecast for themselves without having to rely on reports or updates from the company.

In conclusion, effective communication of cash flow forecasts to stakeholders is crucial for maintaining transparency, building trust, and making informed decisions. By utilizing the tips and strategies outlined in this chapter, businesses can develop strong relationships with stakeholders and drive long-term success. Keep in mind that effective communication is an ongoing process and should be regularly evaluated and improved upon to ensure its effectiveness.

Chapter 24: Monitoring Cash Flow Performance

Key Performance Indicators for Cash Flow

When it comes to managing cash flow, it is important to have a set of key performance indicators (KPIs) in place to track and measure the health of your cash flow. KPIs are financial metrics that can provide valuable insights into your cash flow management. By regularly monitoring and analyzing these KPIs, you can better understand the strengths and weaknesses of your cash flow and make informed decisions to improve it. One important KPI for cash flow is the operating cash flow ratio. This measures the amount of cash generated from operating activities as a percentage of total operating costs. A high operating cash flow ratio indicates a healthy cash flow, while a low ratio may signal potential cash flow issues.

Another important KPI is the cash conversion cycle, which measures the time it takes for a company to convert its inventory into sales and then collect payment from customers. A shorter cash conversion cycle means a company is able to generate cash more quickly, while a longer cycle may indicate a need for improvement in processes.

Analyzing Performance and Making Adjustments

After identifying your KPIs, it is crucial to regularly analyze and track their performance. This will help you identify any patterns or trends in your cash flow and allow you to make necessary adjustments before any issues arise. One effective tool for analyzing cash flow performance is cash flow forecasting. By creating projections of your cash flow based on historical data and future expectations, you can anticipate potential cash flow issues and make adjustments to prevent them.

In addition, regularly reviewing and analyzing your company's financial statements can provide valuable insights into your cash flow performance. Comparing your actual results to your forecasted results can help you identify any discrepancies and make necessary adjustments.

Maintaining Long-Term Growth

While it is important to focus on short-term cash flow management, it is equally important to maintain long-term cash flow stability for sustainable growth. This requires proactive planning and strategic decision-making. One way to maintain long-term growth is by implementing a cash flow contingency plan. This involves identifying potential cash flow disruptions and having a plan in place to mitigate their impact. Such disruptions could include a decrease in sales, unexpected expenses, or changes in market conditions. Another important aspect of maintaining long-term growth is effective cash flow communication. Regularly communicating cash flow goals and expectations with key stakeholders, such as investors and lenders, can help maintain their confidence in your company's financial stability. Furthermore, regularly reviewing and updating your cash flow forecasting and budgeting processes can also help ensure long-term growth. As your company evolves, it is important to adapt these processes to reflect any changes in your business and industry.

In conclusion, monitoring cash flow performance is crucial for the success of any business. By identifying key performance indicators, regularly analyzing results, and maintaining long-term growth, businesses can mitigate potential cash flow issues and set themselves up for sustainable success.

Chapter 25: Cash Flow Forecasting Best Practices - Key Strategies for Success

Key Practices for Accurate Forecasts

Cash flow forecasting is not a one-time exercise, but rather an ongoing process that requires constant monitoring and adjusting. In order to ensure accurate forecasts, it is important to establish key practices from the start. These practices will serve as the foundation for your cash flow forecasting strategy and help guide you towards success.

1. Use historical data: The best way to predict future cash flow is by looking at your past performance. Use historical data to identify trends, patterns, and potential risks that could impact your cash flow. This will help you make more accurate forecasts and plan accordingly.

2. Incorporate variability: Cash flow is not always predictable, and there may be fluctuations due to various factors such as seasonality, economic conditions, or unexpected events. It is important to account for these variables in your forecasting models to ensure more accurate predictions.

3. Utilize multiple scenarios: Instead of relying on a single forecast, consider creating multiple scenarios based on different assumptions. This will give you a better understanding of the potential outcomes and help you prepare for different situations.

4. Involve key stakeholders: Cash flow forecasting should not be done in isolation. Involve key stakeholders, such as your finance team, sales team, and suppliers, in the process to gain valuable insights and identify potential issues that may impact your cash flow.

5. Update forecasts regularly: Cash flow forecasts are only as good as the data and assumptions they are based on. Make sure to update your forecasts regularly to reflect any changes in your business or the market. This will help you stay on top of your finances and make more informed decisions.

Strategies for Continuous Improvement

As with any business process, there is always room for improvement when it comes to cash flow forecasting. By continuously reviewing and refining your strategies, you can make your forecasts more accurate and effective in managing your cash flow. Here are some key strategies for continuous improvement:

1. Track actual vs. forecasted results: It is important to compare your actual cash flow with your forecasted cash flow on a regular basis. This will help you identify any discrepancies and adjust your forecasting strategies accordingly.

2. Use technology: With the advancement of technology, there are now various tools and software available to help with cash flow forecasting. These tools can automate the process, provide real-time data, and offer more advanced forecasting capabilities.

3. Get feedback from stakeholders: As mentioned earlier, involving key stakeholders in the forecasting process is crucial. Make sure to gather feedback from them on the accuracy of your forecasting and any areas for improvement.

4. Analyze and adjust your assumptions: Assumptions play a major role in cash flow forecasting. Make sure to regularly review and analyze your assumptions and adjust them as needed. This will help you make more accurate predictions.

5. Conduct regular training: It is important to ensure that your finance team is equipped with the necessary skills and knowledge to perform effective cash flow forecasting. Conduct regular training to keep them updated on best practices and new techniques.

Common Pitfalls to Avoid

While there are numerous benefits to cash flow forecasting, there are also some common pitfalls that can hinder its effectiveness. These pitfalls can lead to inaccurate forecasts and cause financial difficulties for your business. Here are some common pitfalls to avoid:

1. Ignoring historical data: As mentioned earlier, historical data is crucial in making accurate forecasts. Ignoring this data or not giving it enough weight can result in unreliable predictions.

2. Not accounting for timing differences: Timing differences between cash inflows and outflows can have a major impact on your cash flow. Make sure to account for these differences in your forecasting models.

3. Over/underestimating expenses: Careful attention must be paid to expenses in the forecasting process. Overestimating expenses can result in unnecessary liquidity issues, while underestimating them can lead to financial crises.

4. Neglecting to involve stakeholders: Stakeholders provide valuable insights and perspectives that can greatly impact your cash flow. Neglecting to involve them in the forecasting process can lead to blind spots and missed opportunities.

5. Failing to review and update forecasts: As mentioned earlier, regular review and updates are crucial for accurate forecasting. Failing to do so can result in outdated forecasts that do not reflect current business conditions.

Incorporating these key practices, strategies for continuous improvement, and avoiding common pitfalls will help ensure successful cash flow forecasting. Remember, effective cash flow management is the key to financial stability and growth for your business, and accurate forecasting is a powerful tool in achieving that. Keep learning, adapting, and refining your forecasting strategies, and you will see the positive impact on your business's cash flow.

Chapter 26: Outsourcing Cash Flow Forecasting

Benefits and Risks of Outsourcing

Outsourcing has become a popular business practice in recent years, as companies look for ways to streamline their operations and reduce costs. And when it comes to cash flow forecasting, outsourcing can offer numerous benefits.

But with any decision comes risks, and it's important to carefully consider both sides before deciding to outsource your cash flow forecasting
. Let's take a look at some of the benefits and risks of outsourcing cash flow forecasting.

Benefits:
- Cost Savings:
Outsourcing cash flow forecasting can help save costs in the long run. By partnering with an external provider, companies can avoid hiring additional staff and investing in expensive forecasting software. This creates significant cost savings for businesses of all sizes.

- Expertise and Experience:
Finding, hiring, and training employees to handle cash flow forecasting can be a time-consuming and costly process. Outsourcing allows companies to tap into the expertise and experience of professionals who are dedicated to this specific task, ensuring accurate and efficient forecasting.

- Real-Time Data Analysis:
Outsourcing cash flow forecasting can give companies access to real-time data analysis. This means they can make informed and strategic decisions based on up-to-date information, improving their overall cash flow management.

- Time Savings:
Cash flow forecasting can be a time-sensitive task, and outsourcing it allows companies to focus on their core operations and save time. This can lead to increased productivity and efficiency.

Risks:
- Loss of Control:
One of the biggest risks of outsourcing is losing control over the forecasting process. Companies may feel that they have less control over their finances and may be hesitant to rely on an external provider for such an important task.

- Confidentiality Concerns:
Companies may have concerns about sharing confidential financial information with an external provider. This can include sensitive data such as cash flow projections and financial statements. It's crucial to carefully choose a trusted partner and have a confidentiality agreement in place to address these concerns.

- Communication Challenges:
Effective communication is essential in cash flow forecasting. If there are any communication challenges between the company and the outsourced provider, it could lead to inaccurate forecasts, potentially creating financial problems for the business.

Finding the Right Partner

Outsourcing cash flow forecasting requires significant trust and understanding between the company and the external provider.

To ensure a successful partnership, it's crucial to find the right partner who shares your company's values and has the expertise and experience to meet your specific forecasting needs. Here are some tips for finding the right partner:

- Research and Review:
Do your research and review potential providers carefully. Look into their track record, experience, and areas of expertise. Consider reading client reviews and testimonials for more insight into their services.

- Industry Experience:
Look for a provider who has experience in your industry. It's important to have someone who understands the unique challenges and intricacies of your business, as well as industry regulations and trends.

- Communication and Transparency:
Effective communication is key to a successful partnership. Look for a provider who prioritizes communication and is transparent in their processes.

- Scalability:
Your company's needs may change over time, and it's important to partner with a provider who can adapt and scale their services accordingly.

- Costs and Contracts:
Consider budget and contract terms when choosing a partner. Make sure you understand the costs involved and have a clear understanding of the services provided in the contract.

Developing a Partnership for Long-Term Success

In order to reap the full benefits of outsourcing cash flow forecasting, it's important to develop a strong partnership for long-term success. This includes establishing clear communication channels, setting expectations, and regularly reviewing the provider's performance. Here are some key tips for developing a successful partnership:

- Communication:
Clear and open communication is essential. Make sure to establish communication channels and schedules, and address any concerns or issues that may arise promptly.

- Setting Expectations:
Setting expectations and goals from the start can help ensure that both parties are on the same page. This includes timelines, deliverables, and any specific requirements.

- Regular Reviews:
It's important to regularly review the performance of the outsourced provider. This can help identify any areas for improvement and ensure that the partnership remains beneficial for both parties.

- Collaboration:
While the outsourced provider may handle the cash flow forecasting, it's important for the in-house finance team to still be involved and collaborate with the provider. This can help ensure accurate and effective forecasting.

By considering the benefits and risks of outsourcing, finding the right partner, and developing a strong partnership, companies can successfully outsource their cash flow forecasting and reap its numerous benefits. This can lead to improved financial management, cost savings, and increased efficiency for businesses of all sizes.

Chapter 27: Successful Cash Flow Forecasting Case Studies

Cash flow forecasting is an essential tool for every business, regardless of size or industry. It helps to predict and plan for future financial needs and ensure the smooth operation of the organization. But understanding the concept and techniques of cash flow forecasting is not enough. To truly master it, we need to look at real-life examples of successful cash flow forecasting. In this chapter, we will dive into some case studies and learn valuable lessons from businesses that have implemented effective cash flow forecasting strategies.

Real-Life Examples of Successful Cash Flow Forecasting

1. Apple Inc.

Apple Inc. is a multinational technology company that designs, manufactures, and sells consumer electronics, computer software, and online services. It is one of the most valuable companies in the world, with a market capitalization of over $2 trillion. One of the key reasons for the company's success is its accurate cash flow forecasting.

Apple's cash flow forecast includes detailed projections for the next quarter and the full fiscal year. It also includes a rolling projection for the next two years to track the company's long-term financial health. The company revises its forecast regularly based on changing market conditions, new product launches, and other business factors. This allows Apple to make informed decisions about its investments, production, and expansion plans.

2. Netflix

Netflix is a global streaming giant that has revolutionized the entertainment industry. It has over 200 million subscribers worldwide and is known for its original content, such as Stranger Things and The Crown. With such a massive subscriber base, managing cash flow is crucial for Netflix's success.

One of the key factors behind Netflix's successful cash flow forecasting is its use of data analytics. The company collects and analyzes data from its subscribers, such as viewing habits and preferences, to forecast future cash flow accurately. This helps Netflix determine the potential success of new shows or movies and decide on production and marketing budgets accordingly.

3. Starbucks

Starbucks is a multinational coffee chain that has a presence in over 80 countries. It is known for its high-quality, premium coffee and excellent customer service. However, managing cash flow for such a large food and beverage chain can be challenging, especially during the Covid-19 pandemic.

To overcome this challenge, Starbucks implemented a robust cash flow forecasting system that takes into account both short-term and long-term cash projections. This enabled the company to identify potential cash flow issues and take necessary actions to mitigate them. For example, during the pandemic, the company quickly adapted to changing consumer behavior and focused on its drive-thru and delivery services, which helped maintain its cash flow and stay afloat.

Lessons Learned from Case Studies

The case studies mentioned above highlight some crucial lessons that businesses can learn from successful cash flow forecasting strategies.

1. Accuracy is Key

One of the essential elements of successful cash flow forecasting is accuracy. It is vital to use reliable and accurate data and revise the forecast regularly based on changing market conditions. This will enable businesses to make informed decisions about their finances and take necessary actions to avoid cash flow issues.

2. Use Technology and Data Analytics

The case studies of Apple, Netflix, and Starbucks also show the importance of using technology and data analytics in cash flow forecasting. With the advancements in data analytics and forecasting tools, businesses can now make more accurate and detailed predictions about their finances. This helps them plan and budget more effectively, which is crucial for long-term success.

3. Regularly Monitor and Revise the Forecast

Cash flow forecasting is not a one-time task. It is an ongoing process that requires regular monitoring and revision. By updating the forecast regularly, businesses can identify potential cash flow issues and take necessary actions to mitigate them before they become a significant problem.

Conclusion

Successful cash flow forecasting is crucial for the financial health and growth of any business. By studying case studies and learning from real-life examples, businesses can gain valuable insights and implement effective cash flow forecasting strategies. With the advancements in technology and data analytics, the future of cash flow forecasting looks promising, and businesses that adopt these techniques will have a competitive advantage in the market.

Chapter 28: Applying Cash Flow Forecasting Strategies to Personal Finances

A person's personal finances are one of the most important aspects of their life. It determines their ability to achieve their goals and live a comfortable life. However, many people struggle to manage their finances effectively, often falling into debt and financial difficulties. This is where cash flow forecasting comes in. By using strategies and techniques typically used in business cash flow forecasting, individuals can gain better control over their personal finances and achieve financial stability.

Importance of Personal Budgets

The first step in effectively managing personal finances is creating a budget. This may seem like a tedious and restrictive task, but it is essential in achieving financial goals. Creating a personal budget helps individuals track their income and expenses, identify areas where they are overspending, and make necessary adjustments to stay within their means. A budget also allows for better planning and forecasting of future expenses, ensuring that individuals do not run into financial surprises. When creating a personal budget, it is important to include all sources of income, such as salaries, freelance work, and investments. It is also crucial to list all expenses, including fixed expenses like rent, utilities, and insurance, as well as variable expenses like groceries, entertainment, and transportation.

Using Technology for Personal Forecasting

In today's digital age, technology has made it easier for individuals to manage their personal finances. There are numerous budgeting apps and software available that can help with creating and tracking personal budgets. With the use of these tools, individuals can easily input their income and expenses and receive real-time updates on their financial standing. Additionally, technology can also be used for scenario planning in personal cash flow forecasting. By inputting different income and expense scenarios, individuals can forecast their cash flow and make necessary adjustments to their budget accordingly. This allows for better financial planning and avoids any unwelcome surprises in the future.

Strategies for Personal Cash Flow Forecasting

Now that we understand the importance of personal budgets and the use of technology in personal cash flow forecasting, let us explore some effective strategies for achieving financial stability.

1. Prioritize Expenses: When creating a personal budget, it is important to prioritize expenses. Essential expenses like rent, groceries, and utilities should take precedence over non-essential expenses.

2. Focused Saving: Savings should be a top priority in every personal budget. By setting aside a specific amount each month, individuals can build up an emergency fund and save for their future goals.

3. Cut Unnecessary Expenses: It is important to identify and cut down on unnecessary expenses. Small purchases like daily coffees or monthly subscriptions may seem insignificant, but they can add up and impact financial stability.

4. Set Realistic Goals: When setting financial goals, it is crucial to be realistic. This ensures that individuals do not set themselves up for disappointment or become overwhelmed.

5. Review Regularly: Personal budgets and cash flow forecasts should be reviewed regularly, preferably at least once a month. This allows for necessary adjustments and keeps individuals on track with their financial goals.

In Conclusion

Managing personal finances can seem daunting, but with the use of cash flow forecasting strategies, individuals can gain better control over their finances and achieve financial stability. By creating a personal budget, utilizing technology, and implementing effective strategies, individuals can confidently manage their finances and achieve their financial goals. So, take control of your finances and start your personal cash flow forecasting journey today.

Chapter 29: Cash Flow Forecasting for Financial Planning

As we have discussed throughout this book, cash flow forecasting is an essential tool for businesses and individuals alike. It allows for better financial management and decision making by providing a clear picture of expected cash inflows and outflows. In this chapter, we will delve deeper into how cash flow forecasting can be integrated into financial planning to achieve long-term financial goals.

Integrating Cash Flow Forecasts into Financial Plans

Financial plans are the roadmaps that guide us towards our long-term financial goals. These goals can include saving for retirement, purchasing a home, or paying for your child's education. By incorporating cash flow forecasts into these plans, we can ensure that our goals are realistic and achievable. One way to integrate cash flow forecasts into financial plans is by setting up a cash reserve. This cash reserve can act as a buffer for any unexpected expenses or dips in cash flow. By forecasting your cash flow, you can determine the appropriate amount for your cash reserve and make adjustments as needed.

Another strategy is to align your cash flow forecasts with your financial goals. By regularly reviewing your forecasts and adjusting your spending and saving habits, you can make sure that you stay on track to reach your long-term financial goals. This also allows for early identification of any potential cash flow challenges that may hinder your progress towards your goals.

Predictive Budgeting

Budgeting is a crucial aspect of financial planning, and cash flow forecasting can make it even more effective. Traditionally, budgets are based on past expenses and income. However, by incorporating cash flow forecasts into budgeting, we can make more accurate predictions and adjust our budgets accordingly.

Predictive budgeting involves using cash flow forecasts to forecast future income and expenses. This can help identify any potential budgeting challenges and create a more realistic budget that aligns with your financial goals. With predictive budgeting, we can also plan for any major expenses or investments that may impact our cash flow in the future.

Strategies for Reaching Long-Term Financial Goals

Now that we have discussed how cash flow forecasting can be integrated into financial planning, let's explore some specific strategies for reaching long-term financial goals. One effective strategy is to use cash flow forecasting to identify potential areas for cost-cutting. By regularly reviewing your cash flow forecasts, you can identify any unnecessary expenses and adjust your budget accordingly. This can help you save money in the long run and reach your financial goals faster. Another strategy is to monitor your cash flow closely and make necessary adjustments to investment and savings plans. For example, if your cash flow forecast indicates a significant increase in income in the upcoming months, you may want to consider increasing your investment contributions or setting aside more money for savings. Furthermore, cash flow forecasting can also help individuals and businesses to make informed financial decisions. With a clear understanding of expected cash flow, we can make strategic decisions such as expanding our businesses or making large purchases.

In conclusion, by integrating cash flow forecasting into financial planning, individuals and businesses can gain valuable insights and make informed decisions to achieve long-term financial goals. It allows for better budgeting, monitoring, and cost-cutting strategies, ultimately leading to financial success. Regularly reviewing and adjusting your cash flow forecasts can help you stay on track and make necessary changes as your financial goals evolve.

Chapter 30: Incorporating Cash Flow Forecasts into Investment Analysis

When it comes to making investment decisions, having accurate and reliable information is crucial. This is where cash flow forecasting comes into play. As we have discussed in earlier chapters, cash flow forecasting helps businesses and individuals plan and manage their cash flow effectively. However, it is also a valuable tool for evaluating investment opportunities. In this chapter, we will delve deeper into the role of cash flow forecasting in investment analysis and how it can help you make informed and strategic investment decisions.

Incorporating Cash Flow Forecasts into Investment Analysis

Investment analysis involves evaluating the potential risks and returns of a particular investment opportunity. This process is essential for making wise investment decisions and maximizing the returns on your investments. Traditionally, the most common method of evaluating investment opportunities is through analyzing financial statements, such as income and balance sheets. However, these statements only provide a snapshot of a company's financial health at a particular point in time. This is where cash flow forecasting becomes valuable. By incorporating cash flow forecasts into your investment analysis, you are able to get a more comprehensive understanding of a company's financial situation. Cash flow forecasts provide a projection of future cash flows, giving you a better idea of how the company will perform and generate returns in the future. This information is critical in making well-informed investment decisions.

Evaluating Investment Opportunities

One of the key benefits of using cash flow forecasts in investment analysis is the ability to assess potential investment opportunities more accurately. Cash flow forecasts allow you to project potential cash inflows and outflows from a particular investment, giving you a clear idea of the expected returns and potential risks involved. By incorporating these forecasts into your analysis, you can quickly determine whether an investment opportunity aligns with your financial goals and risk tolerance.

Another important aspect of evaluating investment opportunities is the ability to compare different investment options. By using cash flow forecasts, you can assess the potential returns and risks of various investment opportunities, making it easier to select the most suitable option for your portfolio.

Risk Management

Investing always comes with its fair share of risks. However, by using cash flow forecasts in your investment analysis, you are better equipped to manage these risks. Cash flow forecasts give you a clear understanding of a company's cash inflows and outflows, allowing you to identify any potential red flags. For instance, if a company's cash flow forecast shows a consistent decline in cash inflows, this could be a warning sign of financial instability and may not be a sound investment opportunity.

Moreover, by incorporating different scenarios into your cash flow forecasts, you can also assess the potential impact of external factors, such as economic downturns or industry-specific challenges, on a company's cash flow. This allows you to make more strategic investment decisions, taking into account potential risks and developing contingency plans to mitigate them.

Conclusion

Incorporating cash flow forecasts into your investment analysis allows you to make more informed, well-rounded investment decisions. By providing a projection of future cash flows and risks, cash flow forecasting equips you with the necessary information to evaluate investment opportunities accurately. It also enables you to better manage risks and develop contingency plans to safeguard your investments. So, if you want to take your investment analysis to the next level, be sure to incorporate cash flow forecasts into your strategy.

Chapter 31: Financial Management and Cash Flow Forecasting

Integrating Cash Flow Forecasts into Financial Management Processes

Successful financial management is crucial for every business, regardless of its size or industry. It involves planning, organizing, directing, and controlling a company's financial resources to achieve its financial goals. One important tool in financial management is cash flow forecasting. By integrating cash flow forecasts into financial management processes, businesses can make more informed decisions and improve their overall financial health. Cash flow forecasting provides a detailed prediction of a company's future cash flows, allowing businesses to plan ahead and make strategic financial decisions. By incorporating this information into financial management processes, businesses can create a more accurate financial plan, identify potential cash flow gaps, and anticipate any financial challenges they may face.

For example, if a business forecasts a decrease in cash flow in the upcoming quarter, they can actively seek out additional funding sources or cut costs to mitigate the impact on their financial goals. Without proper integration of cash flow forecasts, businesses may not be equipped to handle these changes and can suffer from a lack of liquidity, hindering their financial management processes.

Importance of Timely and Accurate Cash Flow Information

Timing and accuracy are crucial when it comes to cash flow forecasting. The information used to create forecasts must be up-to-date and reflect the most current financial situation of a company. This allows businesses to make timely and informed decisions that can positively impact their financial management processes. Additionally, accurate cash flow information enables businesses to identify potential cash flow gaps and make necessary adjustments to prevent any financial difficulties. Without this information, businesses may be caught off guard by unexpected expenses or delays in accounts receivable, which can disrupt their financial management processes. Moreover, timely and accurate cash flow information can aid in developing realistic financial goals and budgets. By understanding their current and projected cash flow, businesses can set achievable financial targets and create a plan to reach them. This also allows for more effective monitoring and analysis of a company's financial performance, allowing for adjustments to be made if necessary. Integrating timely and accurate cash flow information into financial management processes also promotes transparency and accountability within a company. By having a clear understanding of their cash flow, businesses can accurately assess their performance and hold their teams accountable for meeting financial targets and staying within budget. In summary, the integration of cash flow forecasting into financial management processes is crucial for businesses to effectively manage their finances. By incorporating this valuable tool, businesses can make better financial decisions, mitigate potential risks, and improve their overall financial health.

Chapter 32: Developing Cash Flow Forecasting Strategies

Key Elements of a Successful Strategy

In a constantly evolving business landscape, having a comprehensive and effective cash flow forecasting strategy is crucial for the success of any organization. But what are the key elements that make up a successful cash flow forecasting strategy? Let's explore some of the most important elements that should be included in your strategy.

Accurate and Timely Data

The first and most crucial element of a successful cash flow forecasting strategy is having access to accurate and timely data. Without up-to-date information on your company's cash inflows and outflows, it is impossible to make accurate predictions and forecasts. Utilizing reliable accounting software and other tools can help to ensure that your data is accurate and readily available at all times.

Clear and Realistic Goals

A successful cash flow forecasting strategy should have clear and realistic goals that align with your business objectives. These goals should be specific, measurable, achievable, relevant, and time-bound (SMART). Having a clear understanding of what you want to achieve through your cash flow forecasting can help guide your strategy and keep you on track towards your goals.

Flexibility and Adaptability

With the ever-changing business landscape, it is essential to have a cash flow forecasting strategy that is flexible and adaptable. Your strategy should be able to accommodate unexpected changes in market conditions, supply chain disruptions, unexpected expenses, or any other external factors that may impact your cash flow. This flexibility will ensure that your forecasts remain accurate and relevant, even amidst unforeseen circumstances.

Risk Management Plan

Cash flow forecasting is not just about predicting your cash inflows and outflows; it's also about managing risks. Your strategy should have a risk management plan in place, outlining potential risks that may affect your cash flow and how to mitigate or address them. This will help you be proactive in managing potential risks and minimize their impact on your cash flow.

Aligning Strategies with Business Goals

Without alignment between your cash flow forecasting strategy and your overall business goals, it becomes challenging to achieve success. Your cash flow strategy should align with your company's short-term and long-term objectives and reflect your organization's overall vision and mission. This alignment ensures that your cash flow forecasting efforts contribute to the growth and success of your business.

Collaboration Across Departments

To align your cash flow forecasting strategy with your business goals, collaboration across departments is crucial. Your finance team cannot work in a silo when it comes to cash flow forecasting. They must collaborate with other departments such as sales, operations, and procurement to gain a holistic view of the company's cash flow. This collaboration will help identify potential discrepancies and enable better forecasting accuracy.

Regular Review and Updates

As your business evolves, so should your cash flow forecasting strategy. Therefore, it is essential to regularly review and update your strategy to ensure it aligns with your business goals. As you achieve your objectives, it may be necessary to set new targets or adjust your cash flow forecasting approach. A thorough review process can help identify areas for improvement and keep your strategy aligned with your business goals.

Continuously Improving Strategies

Finally, a successful cash flow forecasting strategy is not a one-and-done task. It requires continuous improvement to adapt to changing market conditions and business growth. Here are some ways to continuously improve your cash flow forecasting strategy:

Seeking External Expertise

It can be helpful to seek external expertise when developing or improving your cash flow forecasting strategy. Consulting with financial experts can provide valuable insights and help you identify potential blind spots in your strategy. They can also offer suggestions for improvement and best practices from their experience working with similar companies.

Utilizing Technology

Technology plays a vital role in streamlining and improving cash flow forecasting. By utilizing advanced financial software, you can automate the data collection and forecasting process, freeing up time for your finance team to focus on analysis and strategy development. Technology can also help identify patterns and trends in your cash flow data to improve accuracy and decision-making.

Regular Training and Education

To continuously improve your cash flow forecasting strategy, it is essential to invest in regular training and education for your finance team. Stay updated on industry best practices and new developments in technology to ensure your strategy remains relevant and effective.

In conclusion, developing a successful cash flow forecasting strategy is crucial for the financial health and growth of your business. By incorporating accurate data, clear goals, flexibility, and continuously improving your strategy, you can make better-informed decisions and achieve your business goals. Remember to regularly review and update your strategy to stay aligned with your business goals and adapt to changes in the market. With the right strategy in place, you can confidently navigate the ever-changing landscape and achieve success in cash flow forecasting.

Chapter 33: Planning for Cash Flow Disruptions

Identifying Potential Disruptions

Cash flow forecasting is an essential tool for any business owner or manager. It helps to predict future cash inflows and outflows, allowing for better financial planning and decision making. However, even with the most accurate forecasts, unexpected disruptions can occur that can significantly impact a business's cash flow.

As a business owner, it is crucial to identify potential disruptions that may affect your company's cash flow. This can include changes in market trends, unexpected economic downturns, or even natural disasters. By recognizing these potential disruptions, you can prepare for them and minimize their impact on your business's financial stability.

Developing Contingency Plans

One of the best ways to prepare for potential cash flow disruptions is to develop contingency plans. These plans should outline the necessary steps to take in case of a disruption, such as a decrease in sales or a disruption in the supply chain. By having these plans in place, you can quickly respond to unexpected changes and keep your business afloat. When developing contingency plans, it is essential to consider different scenarios and their potential impact on your business. It may also be helpful to consult with your team and financial advisors to ensure that all possible disruptions have been considered.

Importance of Flexibility

In addition to contingency plans, another crucial factor in managing cash flow disruptions is flexibility. As the business landscape continues to evolve and change, it is vital to be adaptable and adjust your strategies accordingly. This flexibility can also apply to your forecasted cash flow. Revising and updating your forecast regularly can help you stay on top of any potential disruptions and make timely adjustments to your financial plans. Another way to maintain flexibility in your cash flow management is by establishing open communication channels within your business. Encouraging your team to share their ideas and concerns can lead to innovative solutions and proactive measures to address any potential disruptions.

Being flexible also means being open to new opportunities for generating income. During times of financial uncertainty, it is essential to explore new revenue streams and leverage existing assets for maximum profitability.

Conclusion

While no business owner wants to think about potential disruptions, it is crucial to be prepared for any unforeseen circumstances that may impact your cash flow. By identifying potential disruptions, developing contingency plans, and maintaining flexibility, you can minimize the impact of these disruptions on your business's financial stability. Remember, cash flow forecasting is a powerful tool, but it is only one part of managing a successful business. So stay vigilant, stay prepared, and stay flexible to navigate any potential cash flow disruptions confidently.

Chapter 34: Cash Flow Forecasting and Financial Forecasting

Relationship Between Cash Flow and Financial Forecasts

Cash flow forecasting and financial forecasting go hand in hand when it comes to planning and managing the financial health of a business. A financial forecast is an estimation of the future performance of a business based on past and current data. It includes projections of revenues, expenses, and profits, and is essential for budgeting and strategic decision making. On the other hand, cash flow forecasting is a prediction of the cash inflows and outflows of a business over a specific period of time. These two types of forecasts are closely related and can greatly impact each other. One of the main reasons for the close relationship between cash flow and financial forecasts is that cash flow is the lifeblood of a business. A company can have a profitable financial forecast, but if there is not enough cash to cover expenses and pay debts, the business can still fail. This is why cash flow forecasting is crucial in the decision-making process, as it provides a more accurate picture of a company's financial situation. Moreover, cash flow forecasts can also help businesses identify potential cash flow gaps in their financial forecast. For example, if a business is expecting a significant increase in revenue in the next quarter, but its cash flow forecast shows a projected decrease in cash, this could indicate a problem with collecting payments or managing inventory. By incorporating cash flow forecasts into financial forecasts, businesses can identify and address these issues before they become a larger problem.

Another important aspect of the relationship between cash flow and financial forecasts is liquidity. A company's liquidity refers to its ability to meet financial obligations in a timely manner. A healthy cash flow is essential for maintaining liquidity, and without it, a company may struggle to pay bills, meet payroll, or invest in growth opportunities. By including cash flow forecasts in financial forecasting, businesses can ensure that they have enough cash on hand to maintain their liquidity and continue operations.

Incorporating Cash Flow Forecasts into Financial Forecasts

Now that we understand the relationship between cash flow and financial forecasts, let's explore how businesses can effectively incorporate cash flow forecasts into their financial planning. The first step is to ensure that both forecasts are aligned in terms of time frame. Typically, financial forecasts cover a longer period, such as a year, while cash flow forecasts focus on a shorter time frame, such as a month or a quarter. By aligning these time frames, businesses can have a more accurate picture of their financial position and make more informed decisions. Next, businesses should regularly update their cash flow forecast with actual data to identify any discrepancies between projected and actual cash flows. This will not only help in making adjustments to the forecast for future periods but also in identifying any areas of improvement in the business's cash flow management. It's also important to involve all relevant departments when creating and updating cash flow and financial forecasts. This includes sales, marketing, operations, and finance teams. This collaboration can provide valuable insights and inputs to make the forecasts more accurate and realistic. One effective way to incorporate cash flow forecasts into financial forecasts is by using scenario planning. Scenario planning involves creating different projections based on different assumptions or events that may occur. For example, a business can create a scenario for a decrease in sales or an unexpected increase in expenses. By incorporating cash flow forecasts into these scenarios, businesses can see how these events would impact their cash flow and financial position, allowing them to plan and prepare accordingly. Another strategy for incorporating cash flow forecasts into financial forecasts is by regularly reviewing and analyzing the forecasts. This can help businesses identify trends, patterns, and any potential issues that may arise. These insights can then be used to make adjustments to future forecasts and ensure that the business is on track to achieve its financial goals.

In conclusion, cash flow forecasting and financial forecasting are closely intertwined and are both essential in managing a business's financial health. By understanding the relationship between these two types of forecasts and incorporating cash flow forecasts into financial forecasts, businesses can make more informed decisions and ensure their long-term success.

Chapter 35: Cash Flow Forecasting for Managing Crisis Situations

Cash flow disruptions can strike any business at any time and can have crippling consequences if not handled properly. In today's ever-changing business landscape, it is crucial for companies to have efficient cash flow forecasting and management strategies in place to handle disruptions and emergencies. In this chapter, we will discuss the importance of crisis management plans and explore effective strategies for handling cash flow disruptions to ensure the stability and success of your business.

Strategies for Handling Cash Flow Disruptions and Emergencies

The key to successfully managing cash flow disruptions and emergencies is to have a proactive approach. For starters, it is essential to have a reliable cash flow forecasting system in place to identify potential problems and plan accordingly. Here are some strategies to help you handle cash flow disruptions and emergencies:

1. Build a Cash Reserve
Building a cash reserve is one of the smartest ways to prepare for any cash flow emergency. A cash reserve can act as a buffer during times of crises, providing you with a financial safety net to keep your business afloat. As a general rule of thumb, it is advisable to have at least three to six months' worth of expenses saved in your cash reserve.

2. Monitor and Analyze Cash Flow Regularly
Regularly monitoring and analyzing your cash flow can help you identify potential disruptions in advance. By tracking your cash flow, you can spot any patterns or trends and adjust your operations accordingly. This will also help you gauge whether your business is on track to meet its targets or if unforeseen expenses may hinder your cash flow.

3. Negotiate with Creditors
In the event of a cash flow disruption, it is crucial to communicate with your creditors to negotiate more favorable terms. This could include extending payment deadlines or

adjusting interest rates. By having open and honest communication with your creditors, you can buy yourself some time and alleviate immediate cash flow issues.

4. Consider Alternative Payment Options
Another helpful strategy for managing cash flow disruptions is to offer alternative payment options to your customers. You could provide discounts for early payments or implement a subscription-based payment plan for long-term customers. These options can help ensure a steady and more predictable cash flow.

5. Increase Cash Inflows
During emergencies, finding ways to increase cash inflows can be crucial for maintaining your business operations. This could include offering sales promotions, upselling or cross-selling to existing customers, or reaching out to new markets. By boosting your cash inflows, you can mitigate the impact of any cash flow disruptions.

Importance of Crisis Management Plans

As the saying goes, "Failing to plan is planning to fail." This applies to managing cash flow disruptions and emergencies as well. Having a well-thought-out crisis management plan in place can make all the difference in how you handle and recover from unexpected financial setbacks. Here are a few reasons why crisis management plans are crucial for businesses:

1. Quick Response Time
In the event of a cash flow crisis, having a crisis management plan can help you act swiftly and decisively. This will help minimize the impact of the disruption and allow you to get your business back on track as soon as possible.

2. Maintaining Control
Without a crisis management plan, business owners may feel overwhelmed and have a sense of losing control during a financial crisis. A solid plan can give you a sense of direction and keep you in control of the situation.

3. Employee Morale and Customer Trust
In times of crisis, it is essential to have a plan in place to communicate with employees and customers effectively. This will help boost employee morale and maintain customer trust, as they will see that you are proactively handling the situation.

4. Identifying Weaknesses

Crises can reveal any weaknesses in your business operations and processes. By reviewing and updating your crisis management plan after a disruption, you can identify any areas that need improvement and make necessary changes to prevent or handle future crises more efficiently.

Conclusion

In today's fast-paced business environment, cash flow disruptions and emergencies are inevitable. However, with a proactive approach and a well-designed crisis management plan, you can effectively manage these disruptions and ensure the stability of your business. By implementing the strategies discussed in this chapter, you can minimize the negative impact of cash flow disruptions and emerge stronger and more resilient from any crisis. Remember, preparation is key, and having a solid cash flow forecasting and management system in place is the best defense against unforeseen financial challenges.

Chapter 36: Cash Flow Forecasting for Different Industries

Unique Considerations for Various Industries

One of the key factors to consider when it comes to cash flow forecasting is the industry in which a business operates. Different industries have their own unique considerations and challenges when it comes to managing cash flow. Understanding these differences and tailoring cash flow forecasting strategies accordingly can greatly improve the chances of success.

Strategies for Successful Cash Flow Forecasting in Different Environments

In this chapter, we will explore the various industries and their specific considerations when it comes to cash flow forecasting. We will also discuss strategies for successful cash flow forecasting in different environments, taking into account the challenges and opportunities that each industry presents.

Retail Businesses

Retail businesses have a unique challenge when it comes to cash flow forecasting. Depending on the industry, retail businesses may have to deal with seasonal fluctuations, changes in consumer buying habits, and competitive pricing pressures. In order to manage cash flow effectively, retail businesses must have a thorough understanding of their inventory turnover and sales cycles. This allows them to accurately predict future cash inflows and outflows, and make necessary adjustments to maintain a healthy cash flow.

Professional Services

For professional service firms, cash flow largely depends on the billing cycle and timely collection of payments. This makes it crucial for these businesses to have an accurate system for forecasting cash flow. In addition, professional service firms must also carefully manage their expenses, as they often have high overhead costs. This requires a detailed understanding of the business's operating expenses and incorporating them into the cash flow forecasting process.

Technology Companies

Technology companies face a unique challenge when it comes to cash flow forecasting due to the nature of their business. These companies often have high upfront costs for research and development, as well as ongoing expenses for maintaining and updating their products or services. At the same time, their revenue streams may be unpredictable, as they rely heavily on sales and long-term contracts. Effective cash flow forecasting for technology companies requires a thorough understanding of their revenue and expenses, as well as continuously monitoring and adjusting forecasts as market conditions change.

Healthcare Organizations

The healthcare industry has its own set of challenges when it comes to cash flow forecasting. Healthcare organizations must navigate complex payment systems and insurance reimbursements, making it difficult to accurately predict future cash flows. In addition, many healthcare organizations face fluctuations in demand for services and must carefully manage their expenses. Successful cash flow forecasting in this industry requires a deep understanding of all financial data, as well as the ability to adapt quickly to changing market conditions.

Transportation and Logistics Companies

For transportation and logistics companies, cash flow forecasting is crucial for managing the costs associated with operating a fleet. These businesses must account for expenses such as fuel, maintenance, and labor, as well as fluctuations in demand and the cost of goods. This requires a detailed understanding of the business's operating costs, as well as forecasting future demand for services. Additionally, transportation and logistics companies must be able to quickly adjust their forecasts in response to unforeseen circumstances, such as changes in regulations or fuel prices.

Agriculture Businesses

Agriculture businesses face a unique challenge when it comes to cash flow forecasting due to the cyclical nature of their operations. These businesses must manage expenses throughout the year, including labor and equipment costs, while waiting for the harvest season to generate revenue. Cash flow forecasting for agriculture businesses requires a thorough understanding of their production and sales cycles, as well as the ability to anticipate and manage potential risks, such as crop failures or fluctuations in market prices.

Hospitality Industry

The hospitality industry relies heavily on seasonal demand for their services, making cash flow forecasting a crucial aspect of their financial management. These businesses must carefully manage expenses, such as labor and inventory costs, during off-peak seasons and anticipate and prepare for spikes in demand during peak seasons. By accurately forecasting cash flow, hospitality businesses can make the necessary adjustments to ensure they have enough liquidity to cover expenses during slow periods and take advantage of opportunities during peak seasons.

Education Institutions

Education institutions, such as schools and universities, have a unique set of considerations when it comes to cash flow forecasting due to their reliance on tuition payments and funding from government agencies. These businesses must carefully manage expenses, such as faculty salaries and facility maintenance costs, while also accounting for potential delays in payments or changes in funding. By accurately predicting cash flow, education institutions can ensure they have enough funds to cover their expenses and provide high-quality education.

Government Agencies

Similar to education institutions, government agencies must carefully manage expenses while also accounting for potential delays in funding. Cash flow forecasting is crucial for these organizations to ensure they have enough funds to fulfill their duties and provide essential services to the public. In addition, forecasting can help identify potential risks or gaps in funding, allowing governments to make necessary adjustments and prioritize allocations.

International Aid Organizations

International aid organizations face unique challenges in cash flow forecasting due to the unpredictable nature of their funding sources. These organizations rely on donations and grants, which can often be affected by global economic or political conditions. As a result, forecasting for these organizations must take into account potential fluctuations in funding and adapt to changing conditions in different countries. Effective cash flow management is essential for these organizations to fulfill their missions and help those in need around the world.

Utilities and Energy Companies

Cash flow forecasting is crucial for utilities and energy companies, which must manage their operations and plan for infrastructure upgrades while also maintaining affordable pricing for customers. These businesses must carefully monitor their expenses, such as fuel and maintenance costs, while also anticipating and budgeting for potential regulatory changes. Cash flow forecasting allows these organizations to balance the needs of their customers with their own financial stability.

Conclusion

Understanding the unique considerations for different industries is essential for successful cash flow forecasting. By tailoring strategies to specific industries and environments, businesses can better manage their cash flow and ensure sustainability and growth. Effective cash flow forecasting requires a thorough understanding of all financial data and the ability to adapt and adjust forecasts as market conditions change. By incorporating these considerations into their forecasting process, businesses can improve their financial management and increase their chances of success.

Chapter 37: Real Estate Cash Flow Forecasting

Real estate can be a lucrative industry, but it also comes with its own unique set of challenges. From unpredictable market trends to changing regulations, real estate professionals must be able to navigate through various obstacles to maintain a stable cash flow. In this chapter, we will discuss key considerations for real estate cash flow forecasting, strategies for maintaining stable cash flow, and the importance of market trends.

Key Considerations for Real Estate Cash Flow Forecasting

Cash flow forecasting is a crucial aspect of financial management in the real estate industry. It involves predicting the inflow and outflow of cash for a specific period, typically on a monthly or quarterly basis. This allows real estate professionals to better manage their finances and make informed decisions. However, there are certain considerations that must be taken into account when creating a cash flow forecast for real estate. One of the key considerations is the timing of cash flows. In the real estate industry, cash flow can be impacted by factors such as rental payments, mortgage payments, and property maintenance expenses. These cash flows may not always align with each other, and it is important to accurately forecast the timing of these inflows and outflows to avoid any potential cash shortages. In addition, real estate professionals must also consider potential cash flow disruptions, such as unexpected repairs or vacancies. These disruptions can have a significant impact on cash flow and must be factored into the forecast. Furthermore, changes in interest rates and inflation also need to be taken into account, as they can affect rental rates and property values. Another crucial consideration is the type of real estate project. For instance, cash flow forecasting for commercial properties may differ from residential properties due to varying rental agreements and expenses. It is important to understand the differences and tailor the forecast accordingly.

Strategies for Maintaining Stable Cash Flow

Maintaining a stable cash flow is vital for the success of any real estate business. One of the most effective strategies is to diversify your portfolio. By investing in a variety of properties, you can spread out the risk and avoid relying too heavily on one specific property or market. Another strategy is to manage expenses carefully. This includes monitoring costs such as property maintenance, taxes, and insurance to ensure they are in line with the projected cash flow. Moreover, staying on top of rent collection and enforcing lease agreements can also help maintain a stable cash flow.

Real estate professionals should also consider exploring different financing options, such as loans or partnerships, to support their cash flow. Finally, having a contingency plan in place for unexpected disruptions can help minimize the impact on cash flow.

Importance of Market Trends

The real estate industry is heavily influenced by market trends, making it crucial for professionals to keep a close eye on them. These trends include factors such as interest rates, housing demand, and economic conditions. For example, rising interest rates can impact the affordability of properties, potentially leading to a decrease in demand. Similarly, economic conditions, such as a recession, can lead to a decrease in property values and rental rates. By monitoring these trends, real estate professionals can adjust their cash flow forecast accordingly and make informed decisions to mitigate any potential risks. In addition, market trends can also present opportunities for real estate professionals to capitalize on. By identifying emerging trends, such as a demand for sustainable housing, professionals can cater to these demands and potentially increase their profits.

In conclusion, cash flow forecasting is a crucial aspect of financial management in the real estate industry. By carefully considering key factors, implementing effective strategies, and staying informed about market trends, professionals can maintain a stable cash flow and achieve success in this ever-changing industry.

Chapter 38: Cash Flow Forecasting for Construction Projects

Construction projects require significant financial resources and careful planning to ensure their successful completion. Cash flow forecasting is crucial in this industry, as it helps contractors and project managers monitor and manage the flow of funds throughout the project's lifecycle. However, there are specific challenges that construction companies face when trying to forecast cash flow accurately. In this chapter, we will explore these challenges and provide strategies for preventing cash flow issues in construction projects.

Challenges in Cash Flow Forecasting for Construction

Cash flow forecasting for construction projects can be complicated due to the long-term nature of these projects, as well as the various stakeholders involved, such as contractors, subcontractors, suppliers, and clients. Here are some common challenges faced by construction companies when forecasting cash flow:

1. Long-Term Nature of Projects

Unlike most businesses where cash flow can be forecasted on a monthly or quarterly basis, construction projects can take months or even years to complete. This makes it challenging to predict future cash inflows and outflows accurately. Changes in the project scope, delays in receiving payments, or unexpected expenses can significantly impact the project's cash flow over time.

2. Dependence on External Factors

Construction projects are susceptible to external factors beyond the control of the company, such as weather conditions, regulatory changes, or economic downturns. These factors can disrupt the project timeline, causing delays or additional costs, which can affect the cash flow forecast.

3. Complex Payment Structures

Construction projects often involve multiple parties with different payment terms and schedules. For example, contractors may be paid based on milestones or the completion of specific tasks, while subcontractors and suppliers may have different payment terms. This complex payment structure makes it challenging to forecast cash flow accurately.

Managing Costs and Timing

To prevent cash flow issues in construction projects, it is essential to manage costs and timing effectively. Here are some strategies that can help:

1. Accurate Cost Estimation

One of the key factors in successful cash flow forecasting for construction projects is the accuracy of cost estimation. It is crucial to estimate all project costs, including materials, labor, equipment, and overhead expenses, as accurately as possible. This will prevent underestimating costs and ensure that enough funds are allocated to cover all project expenses.

2. Regular Cash Flow Monitoring

Construction companies must keep a close eye on their cash flow and monitor it regularly to identify any potential issues, such as delays in receiving payments or unexpected expenses. This will allow them to take action promptly and prevent any significant cash flow disruptions.

3. Streamlining Payment Processes

To simplify the payment process and avoid delays, construction companies can establish consistent payment terms and schedules for all parties involved. This will help avoid confusion and ensure timely payments, improving the project's overall cash flow.

Strategies for Preventing Cash Flow Issues

Apart from managing costs and timing, there are other strategies that construction companies can implement to prevent cash flow issues in their projects. These include:

1. Negotiating Payment Terms

When negotiating contracts with clients, construction companies can include terms that allow for interim or progress payments. This will help maintain a steady cash flow throughout the project's duration, instead of waiting for a lump sum payment at the end.

2. Leveraging Technology

There are various software tools and technology solutions available in the market that can help with cash flow forecasting for construction projects. These tools automate the process, making it more accurate and less time-consuming. They can also provide real-time insights into the project's financial health and flag any potential cash flow issues.

3. Diversifying Revenue Streams

Construction companies can also diversify their revenue streams to reduce their reliance on a single project's cash flow. For example, they can take on smaller projects or offer additional services to generate steady cash flow in between larger projects.

In conclusion, accurate cash flow forecasting is vital for the success of construction projects. By understanding the specific challenges in cash flow forecasting for construction and implementing the strategies mentioned above, companies can prevent cash flow issues and ensure the project's smooth completion.

Chapter 39: Managing Cash Flow for Retail Businesses

Retail businesses are known for facing unique challenges when it comes to managing cash flow. With fluctuating demand and changing consumer trends, it can be difficult to maintain a steady stream of cash throughout the year. This is why proper cash flow forecasting and management is crucial for the success of retail businesses. In this chapter, we will discuss some effective strategies for managing cash flow in the retail industry.

Managing Seasonality

One of the biggest challenges for retailers is the seasonal nature of their business. Many retailers experience a spike in sales during certain times of the year, such as holiday seasons or back-to-school shopping, while experiencing a decline in sales during slower periods. This can greatly impact cash flow, leading to periods of surplus followed by periods of shortage. One way to manage this seasonality is by creating a cash flow plan that takes into account the expected fluctuations in sales. By analyzing past sales data and predicting future trends, retailers can estimate when and how much cash will be needed during peak sales seasons. This allows for more efficient budgeting and preparation for the anticipated increase in sales.

Another effective strategy is to diversify product offerings to reduce reliance on seasonal sales. By expanding the range of products offered, retailers can generate revenue throughout the year rather than relying on one or two peak seasons. This not only helps to stabilize cash flow but also attracts a diverse customer base.

Strategies for Controlling Inventory and Costs

Inventory management and cost control are crucial for maintaining a healthy cash flow in the retail industry. Excess inventory can tie up cash and increase storage and maintenance costs, while insufficient inventory can result in lost sales. It is important for retailers to strike a balance between these two extremes in order to optimize cash flow. One effective strategy is to implement a just-in-time inventory system, where inventory is ordered and stocked based on actual sales rather than on estimates or forecasts. This reduces the risk of overstocking and minimizes the amount of capital tied up in inventory. Additionally, retailers can negotiate with suppliers for better payment terms, such as longer credit periods or discounts for early payments. This can help to improve cash flow by extending the time between paying for inventory and receiving payment from customers. Controlling costs is another important aspect of managing cash flow in the retail industry. Retailers should regularly review their expenses, negotiate better deals with vendors, and eliminate any unnecessary costs. This helps to free up cash for other business needs and ensures that the business is operating at maximum efficiency.

Building Strong Customer Relationships

One of the most valuable assets for retailers is their customer base. Building and maintaining strong relationships with customers can greatly impact cash flow. Loyal customers are more likely to make repeat purchases and are willing to pay a premium for quality products or services. Retailers can focus on building customer loyalty by offering incentives, such as loyalty programs, discounts, or special offers. These not only encourage repeat business but also increase customer satisfaction and build brand loyalty. Another effective strategy is to provide excellent customer service. This includes addressing customer concerns in a timely and satisfactory manner, providing a seamless shopping experience, and creating personalized interactions. By prioritizing customer satisfaction, retailers can build a loyal customer base that generates consistent revenue throughout the year.

In conclusion, effectively managing cash flow is crucial for the success of retail businesses. By understanding and planning for seasonal fluctuations, implementing smart inventory and cost control strategies, and focusing on building strong customer relationships, retailers can achieve a steady stream of cash flow throughout the year. Remember, cash flow forecasting and management should be an ongoing process, constantly reviewed and adjusted as the retail industry is dynamic and ever-changing.

Chapter 40: Cash Flow Forecasting for Professional Services

Cash flow forecasting is crucial for any business, but it is especially crucial for professional service businesses. These businesses often have time-sensitive and variable incomes, making it challenging to create accurate and reliable cash flow projections. However, with the right strategies and techniques, professional service businesses can successfully manage their cash flow and build a solid financial foundation for their operations.

Managing Time-Sensitive and Variable Incomes

One of the biggest challenges for professional service businesses is managing time-sensitive and variable incomes. Unlike traditional businesses that generate consistent revenue through product sales, professional service businesses often rely on invoicing for their income. This means that the timing and consistency of payments can vary greatly from month to month, depending on the projects they are working on. To effectively manage time-sensitive and variable incomes, professional service businesses need to have a clear understanding of their cash flow situation. This can be achieved by regularly reviewing and updating cash flow projections. By incorporating timelines for invoice payments and project completion dates, businesses can better anticipate their cash flow needs and plan accordingly. Another useful strategy for managing time-sensitive and variable incomes is to implement payment terms for services. This can include requiring clients to pay a deposit upfront or setting up installment payment plans. These measures can help to improve cash flow and provide a more consistent income stream.

Strategies for Balancing Cash Flow Between Projects

Professional service businesses often work on multiple projects simultaneously, each with its own payment schedule. This can create cash flow challenges, as income might not align with expenses or the business may have to wait for extended periods before receiving payment. To avoid cash flow imbalances, businesses can implement strategies for balancing cash flow between projects. One effective way to do this is by negotiating payment terms with clients. For example, businesses can offer discounts for early payments or schedule payments at specific intervals throughout the project. This allows for a more consistent and predictable cash flow, making it easier to manage finances.

Another strategy is to diversify services to have a mix of short-term and long-term projects. By having a variety of projects with different payment schedules, businesses can avoid large cash flow gaps and better manage their income and expenses.

Building a Reliable Client Base

One of the most critical factors in maintaining a healthy cash flow for professional service businesses is having a reliable client base. Securing recurring clients or long-term contracts can provide a consistent and predictable income stream, reducing the risk of cash flow challenges. To build a reliable client base, businesses should focus on providing excellent services and building strong relationships with clients. This can include providing exceptional customer service, being responsive to their needs and concerns, and delivering high-quality work consistently. Networking and marketing efforts can also help attract new clients and diversify the client base. Professional service businesses can attend industry events, join networking groups, and invest in targeted marketing campaigns to connect with potential clients and showcase their expertise. Finally, businesses can also explore new opportunities and expand their services to reach new markets and attract more clients. This can open up additional streams of income and create a more stable and diversified client base.

In conclusion, cash flow forecasting is crucial for the success of professional service businesses. By understanding the challenges of time-sensitive and variable incomes, implementing strategies for balancing cash flow between projects, and building a reliable client base, businesses can effectively manage their cash flow and establish a solid financial foundation for their operations. As such, consistent monitoring and updating of cash flow projections and implementing these strategies can help professional service businesses thrive and succeed in their industry.

Book 2 - Extra Strategies

Chapter 41: Successful Cash Flow Forecasting for Technology Companies

Technology companies are often fast-paced and dynamic, with constantly changing markets and business models. This makes cash flow forecasting a crucial aspect of financial management for these organizations. In chapter 41, we will explore the unique challenges and opportunities that technology companies face in cash flow forecasting. From managing revenue and expenses to forecasting long-term expenses and strategies for continuous growth, we will provide you with the knowledge and tools to successfully forecast cash flow for your tech company.

Managing Revenue and Expenses

One of the main challenges for technology companies in cash flow forecasting is managing revenue and expenses. In this ever-evolving industry, businesses must constantly innovate and invest to stay ahead of the competition. This can create fluctuations in revenue and make it difficult to accurately forecast cash flow. To overcome this challenge, tech companies must have a deep understanding of their business model, market trends, and customer needs. To manage revenue, tech companies must have a clear understanding of their sales pipelines and the expected timing of incoming payments. They should also closely monitor market trends and adapt their products or services accordingly to ensure a steady revenue stream. For example, a tech company may forecast an increase in revenue based on the upcoming launch of a new product, but if they fail to deliver on time, their cash flow forecast will be impacted. By closely monitoring their sales pipelines and staying proactive in their approach, tech companies can mitigate the risk of forecasting inaccuracies.

In terms of managing expenses, technology companies must be strategic in their spending. With a plethora of tools, technologies, and services available, it can be tempting for businesses to overspend on unnecessary items. However, by carefully evaluating their expenses and prioritizing investments that align with their business goals, tech companies can better predict and manage their cash flow. This will also enable them to make more informed decisions on when and where to cut costs if needed.

Forecasting for Long-Term Expenses

In addition to managing day-to-day expenses, technology companies must also consider long-term expenses in their cash flow forecasting. These may include investments in research and development, expansion into new markets, or acquiring other businesses. These expenses may not have an immediate impact on cash flow, but they can significantly impact the company's financial health in the long run.

To forecast long-term expenses, tech companies must have a comprehensive understanding of their future goals and plans. This includes analyzing market trends, competitor strategies, and their own capabilities. By looking at the bigger picture and forecasting for potential expenses, businesses can better prepare for future cash flow fluctuations and ensure sustainable growth.

Strategies for Continuous Growth

For tech companies, growth is not just a goal, it is a necessity. This means that cash flow forecasting must not only account for current expenses and revenue but also plan for continuous growth. This can be achieved through strategic financial planning and forecasting for potential opportunities and risks. In order to successfully forecast for growth, tech companies must have a clear understanding of their market and their competitive advantage. By carefully analyzing market trends and their own capabilities, businesses can identify potential growth opportunities and plan for them accordingly. This may include investing in new technologies, expanding into new markets, or diversifying their product offerings. Moreover, businesses must also consider potential risks in their growth plans and prepare for them. This could include having a contingency plan in case of unexpected expenses or fluctuations in revenue. By incorporating potential growth opportunities and risks in their cash flow forecasting, tech companies can better prepare for sustainable and continuous growth.

In conclusion, technology companies face unique challenges in cash flow forecasting, but with the right strategies and tools, they can overcome them and ensure financial success. By closely managing revenue and expenses, forecasting for long-term expenses, and planning for continuous growth, tech companies can confidently make financial decisions that support their vision for the future. Utilize the insights and tips provided in this chapter to take your tech company's cash flow forecasting to the next level.

Chapter 42: Cash Flow Forecasting for Healthcare Organizations

Unique Challenges for Healthcare Cash Flow

The healthcare industry faces a unique set of challenges when it comes to managing cash flow. With constantly changing regulations, shifting reimbursement models, and increasing costs, maintaining a healthy cash flow can be a daunting task for healthcare organizations. However, with the right strategies in place, healthcare providers can stay ahead of the curve and ensure a stable and sustainable cash flow.

Managing Revenue and Expenses

One of the biggest challenges for healthcare cash flow is managing revenue and expenses. In a traditional fee-for-service model, revenue is generated based on the number of services provided. However, with the shift towards value-based reimbursement, healthcare organizations must now focus on delivering quality care at a lower cost. This means that expenses must be carefully managed to ensure profitability, while still maintaining high-quality care for patients. Healthcare providers must also deal with delayed payments from insurance companies, which can significantly impact cash flow. This is where effective cash flow forecasting comes into play. By accurately predicting future revenue and expenses, healthcare organizations can better plan for potential shortfalls and adjust their spending accordingly.

Strategies for Adapting to Changing Regulations

The healthcare industry is no stranger to constantly changing regulations. As new laws and policies are introduced, healthcare organizations must adapt quickly to stay compliant. This can have a major impact on cash flow, as regulations can affect reimbursement rates and billing processes. To navigate these challenges, healthcare providers must have a thorough understanding of the current regulatory landscape and be prepared to adapt their processes as needed. This includes staying up-to-date on changes in reimbursement models, coding and billing guidelines, and documentation requirements. Proactive cash flow management is crucial in times of regulatory change. By regularly reviewing and adjusting cash flow forecasts, healthcare organizations can anticipate any potential changes and mitigate their impact on cash flow.

Strategies for Managing Cash Flow in Uncertain Times

The healthcare industry is also subject to economic uncertainties, such as changes in government policy, economic downturns, and unexpected events like the current global pandemic. These factors can significantly impact both patient volumes and reimbursement rates, making it difficult for healthcare providers to maintain a stable cash flow. To prepare for uncertain times, healthcare organizations must have contingency plans in place. This could include having a cash reserve to cover any unexpected shortfalls, negotiating payment plans with vendors, or even diversifying revenue streams. It's also important to regularly review and update cash flow forecasts to account for any potential risks. Additionally, implementing technology can greatly help with cash flow management in uncertain times. Automating processes such as billing and collections can streamline revenue cycle management and help maintain a steady cash flow.

In conclusion, managing cash flow in the healthcare industry is a complex and ever-changing task. By proactively forecasting and adjusting for potential challenges, healthcare organizations can maintain a healthy cash flow and continue to provide quality care for their patients. With the right strategies in place, healthcare providers can weather any uncertainties and come out stronger on the other side.

Chapter 43: Cash Flow Forecasting for Transportation and Logistics Companies

Dealing with Fluctuations in Fuel Prices

For transportation and logistics companies, fuel prices can have a significant impact on their cash flow. With fuel being one of the major expenses for these companies, any fluctuations in fuel prices can greatly affect their profit margins. As a result, it is important to have strategies in place to deal with these fluctuations and maintain a steady cash flow. One way to deal with fluctuations in fuel prices is by using fuel hedging. This involves locking in a fuel price for a certain period of time, protecting the company from sudden increases in fuel prices. However, fuel hedging can also limit the company's ability to take advantage of decreases in fuel prices. It is important to carefully assess the risks and benefits before implementing a fuel hedging strategy.

Another strategy is to constantly monitor fuel prices and adjust pricing or routes accordingly. Utilizing technology and data analysis can help identify the most cost-efficient routes and pricing strategies based on current fuel prices. This can help offset any increases in fuel prices and maintain a stable cash flow.

Managing Timing Differences in Payments

Transportation and logistics companies often have to deal with timing differences in payments. This is when there is a delay between the time a service is provided and when payment is received. For example, a trucking company may deliver goods to a customer, but the customer may not pay until several weeks later.

To manage these timing differences, companies can implement invoice factoring. This involves selling unpaid invoices to a factoring company for a fee, allowing the company to receive the cash immediately. However, this can also result in a decrease in profit margins. Another solution is to negotiate shorter payment terms with customers or offer discounts for early payments.

Strategies for Maintaining Efficient Cash Flow

Maintaining an efficient cash flow is crucial for transportation and logistics companies, as delays in payment or unexpected expenses can greatly impact their operations. One strategy for efficient cash flow management is to closely monitor expenses and reduce any unnecessary costs. Another effective strategy is to maintain a sufficient level of cash reserves. This ensures that the company has enough funds to cover any unexpected expenses or delays in payment. Setting aside a portion of profits for a cash reserve can help alleviate the stress of cash flow fluctuations. Technology can also play a role in maintaining efficient cash flow. Cash flow forecasting software can help companies accurately predict their cash flow and identify potential issues ahead of time. This allows for better planning and budgeting, minimizing the impact of any unexpected cash flow problems. In addition, strong financial management practices can greatly contribute to efficient cash flow. This includes regularly reviewing financial statements and analyzing key metrics, as well as actively managing accounts receivable and payables to ensure timely payments and collections.

In conclusion, managing cash flow for transportation and logistics companies can be challenging due to factors such as fuel prices and timing differences in payments. However, implementing strategies such as fuel hedging, invoice factoring, and maintaining efficient cash flow can help these companies navigate through these challenges and maintain a strong financial position. By staying proactive and utilizing technology and strong financial management practices, transportation and logistics companies can ensure a stable cash flow and continue to thrive in their industry.

Chapter 44: Cash Flow Forecasting for Agriculture Businesses

Managing Seasonal Expenses

Agriculture businesses are heavily reliant on seasonal factors, from weather conditions to crop cycles. This means that expenses for these businesses tend to fluctuate greatly throughout the year. During peak seasons, expenses may skyrocket as crops need to be planted, maintained, and harvested. On the other hand, during off-seasons, expenses may decrease as there is less work to be done. However, it is important for agriculture businesses to carefully manage these seasonal expenses in order to maintain a healthy cash flow. One strategy for managing seasonal expenses is to create a cash flow budget that takes into account the expected expenses for each season. This can help businesses plan and budget accordingly, ensuring that they have enough cash on hand to cover all expenses. It is also important to track actual expenses against the budget to identify any areas where costs can be reduced. Another strategy is to negotiate with suppliers for better prices during off-seasons. Since most businesses in the agriculture industry experience off-season periods, suppliers may be more willing to offer discounts or negotiate payment terms during these times. This can help reduce expenses and improve cash flow during slower periods.

Strategies for Dealing with Unpredictable Revenue

Aside from seasonal expenses, agriculture businesses also face unpredictable revenue due to factors such as crop yields, market demand, and weather conditions. This can make it difficult to accurately forecast cash flow and plan for expenses. However, there are some strategies that can help mitigate the impact of unpredictable revenue on cash flow. One strategy is to maintain a cash reserve. By setting aside a portion of profits during peak seasons, businesses can create a safety net for slower periods when revenue may be lower. This can help cover expenses and prevent cash flow issues during unpredictable times.

Another strategy is to diversify income streams. Agriculture businesses can explore other avenues for generating revenue, such as selling value-added products or offering agritourism activities. This can help generate income throughout the year, instead of relying solely on revenues from crops.

Importance of Risk Management

When dealing with unpredictable revenue and seasonal expenses, risk management is crucial for agriculture businesses. This involves identifying potential risks and implementing strategies to mitigate or minimize their impact. One risk that agriculture businesses face is crop failure due to weather conditions or pests. By taking preventive measures such as proper crop rotation, irrigation, and pest control, businesses can reduce the risk of crop failure and maintain a steady revenue stream. Another risk is market fluctuations and changes in demand. By regularly monitoring the market and diversifying their products, businesses can adapt to changing market conditions and potentially generate more revenue. Additionally, risk management also involves having insurance coverage for potential risks. This can help protect businesses from financial losses due to crop failure, natural disasters, and other unforeseen events.

In conclusion, managing seasonal expenses, developing strategies for dealing with unpredictable revenue, and implementing risk management practices are essential for cash flow forecasting in agriculture businesses. By carefully planning and preparing for potential cash flow challenges, businesses can maintain a healthy cash flow throughout the year and ultimately, improve their overall financial stability.

Chapter 45: Cash Flow Forecasting for Hospitality Industry

The hospitality industry, including hotels, restaurants, and tourism businesses, is known for its seasonal fluctuations. These businesses often experience high demand during peak seasons, followed by a decline in off-peak periods. It is vital for these businesses to effectively manage cash flow to survive during slower months and make the most of their busy season. In this chapter, we will explore how seasonal variations impact cash flow in the hospitality industry and strategies for improving cash flow management in these businesses.

Accounting for Seasonal Variations

Seasonal variations can significantly impact the cash flow of businesses in the hospitality industry. For example, hotels may experience a surge in reservations and revenue during tourist season, while restaurants in popular vacation destinations may see a decrease in customers during off-peak months. Therefore, it is essential for these businesses to account for these fluctuations in their cash flow forecasts and adjust expenses accordingly. The first step in accounting for seasonal variations is to analyze past years' data and identify patterns. This can help businesses understand which months are typically busy and which are slower. By using this information, businesses can anticipate their cash flow needs and proactively plan for any potential cash flow shortages during slower months. Another approach to accounting for seasonal variations is to have a separate cash flow budget for each season. This budget should take into consideration the expected increase or decrease in sales, as well as any additional expenses, such as increased staffing during peak seasons. By having a clear understanding of their cash flow needs for each season, businesses can make informed decisions and avoid cash flow problems.

Managing Operational Costs

In the hospitality industry, operational costs can significantly impact cash flow. It is crucial for businesses to find ways to manage these costs to maintain a healthy cash flow throughout the year. One strategy for managing operational costs is to negotiate with suppliers for better rates or discounts. By reducing the cost of inventory and supplies, businesses can improve their profit margins and increase cash reserves. Additionally, businesses can leverage technology to automate processes and reduce labor costs. For example, instead of hiring multiple staff members to manage reservations, businesses can invest in a reservation software to handle the task efficiently. Another cost-saving strategy is to re-evaluate pricing strategies during off-peak months. Businesses can offer promotions or discounts to attract customers during slower periods and maintain a steady cash flow.

Strategies for Improving Cash Flow Management in Hotels, Restaurants, and Tourism Businesses

Proper cash flow management is crucial for the survival and success of businesses in the hospitality industry. Here are some strategies these businesses can implement to improve their cash flow management:

- Utilize cash flow forecasting: Cash flow forecasting is an essential tool for managing cash flow in the hospitality industry. It allows businesses to anticipate their cash flow needs and make informed decisions, such as when to invest in equipment or hire seasonal staff. By regularly updating cash flow forecasts, businesses can also proactively plan for any potential cash flow shortages and avoid financial difficulties.

- Implement strict payment policies: To maintain a steady cash flow, businesses should have clear payment policies and enforce them consistently. This can include collecting deposits or implementing penalties for late payments.

- Offer multiple payment options: Providing customers with various payment options, such as credit card, cash, or online payments, can make it easier for them to pay and improve cash flow for businesses.

- Implement cost-cutting measures during slower months: During off-peak seasons, businesses can find ways to reduce expenses and preserve cash reserves. For example, restaurants can reduce their opening hours or hotels can offer reduced amenities to decrease operational costs.

- Negotiate favorable terms with suppliers: Negotiating with suppliers for better rates or payment terms can help reduce costs and improve cash flow for businesses in the hospitality industry.

In conclusion, cash flow management is crucial for the success of businesses in the hospitality industry. By understanding and accounting for seasonal variations, effectively managing operational costs, and implementing strategies for improving cash flow, these businesses can ensure a steady cash flow throughout the year and weather any financial challenges that may arise. With proper cash flow management, hotels, restaurants, and tourism businesses can thrive in both busy and slower seasons.

Chapter 46: Cash Flow Forecasting for Education Institutions

Unique Challenges for Educational Organizations

Education institutions, whether it be schools, universities, or other learning centers, face unique challenges when it comes to managing cash flow. Unlike traditional businesses, their primary source of revenue comes from tuition and other fees paid by students, which are often received sporadically throughout the year. This means that there can be significant fluctuations in cash flow, making it difficult for educational organizations to budget and plan accordingly. In addition to this, educational institutions also have to comply with various regulations and accreditations, which can add to their financial burden. Furthermore, they must constantly invest in technology and resources to keep up with the ever-evolving needs of students and the education industry. All of these factors make cash flow forecasting crucial for the financial stability and success of educational organizations.

Strategies for Budgeting and Managing Cash Flow During Fluctuations

In order to effectively manage cash flow in the unpredictable world of education, here are some strategies that educational organizations can implement:

1. Diversify Income Streams
While tuition and fees are the main source of revenue for educational institutions, it's important to diversify income streams to reduce the impact of fluctuations. This can include offering additional services such as summer programs, online courses, or renting out facilities for events.

2. Create a Cash Reserve
Having a cash reserve can help buffer against any unexpected dips in cash flow. This reserve can be built up by setting aside a portion of surplus funds or through fundraising efforts, such as alumni donations.

3. Utilize Technology

Implementing technology, such as online payment systems and budgeting software, can help streamline the cash flow process and make it more efficient. This can also help with monitoring and tracking expenses, allowing for better financial planning.

4. Monitor and Review Budgets Regularly

With unpredictable cash flow, it's crucial for educational organizations to regularly monitor and review their budgets. This will help identify any areas where expenses can be reduced or reallocated, as well as ensure that the budget aligns with the organization's goals and strategies.

5. Communicate with Stakeholders

Effective communication with stakeholders, including students, parents, staff, and donors, is essential for managing cash flow in an educational institution. This could involve setting clear payment deadlines and offering various payment options to ensure timely payments.

6. Plan for Fluctuations

Educational organizations should also have contingency plans in place in case of any significant fluctuations in cash flow. This could involve seeking out emergency funding sources or cutting back on non-essential expenses.

7. Seek Professional Help

Cash flow forecasting can be a daunting task, especially for organizations that may not have dedicated financial teams. Seeking assistance from professionals, such as accountants or financial advisors, can provide valuable insights and help ensure accuracy in cash flow forecasting.

In conclusion, cash flow forecasting plays a crucial role in the financial stability and success of educational institutions. By understanding the unique challenges they face, and implementing effective strategies, educational organizations can ensure they are able to meet their financial obligations and continue providing quality education to their students.

Chapter 47: Cash Flow Forecasting for Government Agencies

Accounting for Tax Revenue and Expenses

As a government agency, managing cash flow is crucial for carrying out essential functions and providing services to the public. One of the main sources of cash flow for government agencies is tax revenue. It is important to have a clear understanding of when tax revenues will be received and how they will be used to cover expenses. The first step in accounting for tax revenue is to accurately forecast the amount and timing of collections. This can be challenging, as it often depends on economic conditions and changes in tax laws. Utilizing historical data and economic forecasts can aid in creating a reliable tax revenue forecast. Once tax revenue is collected, it is important to plan how it will be used to cover expenses. Some agencies may have restrictions on how tax revenue can be spent, while others may have more flexibility. Careful planning and budgeting can help ensure that tax revenue is used efficiently and effectively to meet the agency's objectives.

Another important consideration when accounting for cash flow in government agencies is the timing of expenses. Government agencies often have fixed expenses, such as payroll and debt payments, but may also have fluctuating expenses based on programs and initiatives. It is crucial to have a clear picture of when these expenses will occur to effectively manage cash flow.

Strategies for Managing Cash Flow During Uncertain Economic Conditions

One of the biggest challenges for government agencies is managing cash flow during uncertain economic conditions. During times of economic downturn, tax revenues may decrease while expenses may increase. In these situations, it is vital for government agencies to have contingency plans in place. One strategy for managing cash flow during uncertain economic conditions is to prioritize expenses and cut non-essential spending. This may involve reevaluating programs and services to determine their necessity and effectiveness. It is important to maintain open communication with employees and stakeholders about any changes and the reasons behind them. Another strategy is to seek out alternative sources of revenue. This may involve applying for grants or collaborating with other agencies to share resources and costs. Additionally, government agencies may look into cost-saving measures, such as negotiating contracts or implementing technology to streamline processes. Effective cash flow management during uncertain economic conditions also involves careful monitoring and analysis. Regularly reviewing cash flow reports and adjusting forecasts can help identify potential issues early on and allow for proactive management.

In addition, government agencies can consider utilizing borrowing and investing strategies to improve cash flow. This may involve issuing short-term notes or investing surplus funds to earn interest.

Conclusion

Managing cash flow for government agencies is a complex and important process. Accounting for tax revenue and expenses, along with implementing strategies to manage cash flow during uncertain economic conditions, is crucial for the smooth operation of government agencies. By utilizing forecasting techniques, effective planning and budgeting, and proactive management, government agencies can maintain stable cash flow and fulfill their responsibilities to the public.

CHAPTER 48: Cash Flow Forecasting for International Aid Organizations

International aid organizations, also known as non-governmental organizations (NGOs), play a crucial role in providing humanitarian assistance to those in need around the world. These organizations rely heavily on donor funds and expenses need to be carefully managed to ensure that aid reaches those who need it most. Accurate cash flow forecasting is essential for NGOs to effectively manage their finances and fulfill their mission. In this chapter, we will explore the unique considerations for NGOs, managing donor funds and expenses, and the importance of accurate cash flow forecasts in humanitarian aid.

Chapter 48: Cash Flow Forecasting For International Aid Organizations

Unique Considerations for NGOs

NGOs operate in a unique environment compared to other businesses and organizations. They often face challenges such as political instability, natural disasters, and armed conflicts, making it difficult to predict and manage cash flow. In addition, NGOs rely heavily on funding from donors, which can be inconsistent and unpredictable. As a result, NGOs must have a comprehensive understanding of their financial situation at all times, making cash flow forecasting a critical tool. One of the main challenges for NGOs is the uncertainty of future funding. Donors may change their priorities or withdraw funding at any time, impacting NGOs' cash flow. This uncertainty makes it crucial for NGOs to have accurate cash flow forecasts to make informed decisions and plan for potential funding gaps.

Another unique consideration for NGOs is the pressure to maximize the impact of donor funds. Unlike for-profit businesses, NGOs must use donor funds efficiently to achieve their missions and provide aid to those in need. This pressure further highlights the importance of accurate cash flow forecasting to ensure that funds are allocated appropriately and effectively.

Managing Donor Funds and Expenses

For NGOs, managing donor funds and expenses is a delicate balancing act. Donors often have specific guidelines on how their funds should be used and require strict reporting on how the money is spent. NGOs must have a transparent and efficient financial management system in place to track and report on the use of donor funds accurately. Cash flow forecasting plays a crucial role in managing donor funds. It allows NGOs to plan and allocate funds according to donors' requirements, ensuring that the funds are used for their intended purpose within the designated time frame. By having a clear understanding of their cash flow, NGOs can avoid overspending or being unable to meet donor obligations.

Expenses must also be carefully managed to ensure that donor funds are not being wasted or misused. Cash flow forecasting helps NGOs to track and monitor expenses, identify areas where costs can be reduced, and allocate funds effectively. This level of financial control is essential for NGOs to maintain the trust and support of their donors.

Importance of Accurate Cash Flow Forecasts in Humanitarian Aid

When providing humanitarian aid, NGOs must act quickly to assist those in need. This sense of urgency makes it even more crucial for NGOs to have accurate cash flow forecasts. It allows them to plan and allocate funds efficiently, ensuring that aid reaches those who need it most in a timely manner. Accurate cash flow forecasts also help NGOs to make informed decisions during crises. For example, if a natural disaster or armed conflict occurs, NGOs can use their forecasts to determine the financial resources they have available and mobilize them to provide immediate aid. Moreover, NGOs must be accountable for the funds they receive and how they are used. Donors want assurance that their funds are being used effectively to provide humanitarian aid. With accurate cash flow forecasting, NGOs can track and report on the use of funds to maintain transparency, credibility, and donor trust.

In conclusion, accurate cash flow forecasting is vital for international aid organizations. NGOs operate in a unique environment and face challenges that require careful financial management. By having a comprehensive understanding of their cash flow, NGOs can make informed decisions, manage donor funds and expenses efficiently, and fulfill their mission of providing humanitarian aid to those in need around the world.

Chapter 49: Strategies for Cash Flow Forecasting in Utilities and Energy Companies

As a Utilities and Energy company, managing cash flow can be a complex and challenging task. There are various factors that can affect your cash flow, from timing differences in billing and payments to unexpected maintenance and unplanned costs. That's why having a solid cash flow forecasting strategy is crucial to the success of your company. In this chapter, we will discuss various strategies for cash flow forecasting in Utilities and Energy companies, and how you can mitigate risks to ensure a steady cash flow.

Managing Timing Differences in Billing and Payments

One of the biggest challenges faced by Utilities and Energy companies is the timing difference between billing and payments. In most cases, companies bill their customers on a monthly basis, but the payment from the customer may not be received until much later. This can create a significant gap in your cash flow, making it difficult to manage expenses and keep the business running smoothly. To manage this challenge, it is important to have a thorough understanding of your billing and payment cycles. Analyze your past billing and payment trends to identify any patterns or delays. This will help you create a more accurate cash flow forecast and anticipate any potential gaps. Another strategy is to incentivize customers to pay early or on time. Offer discounts or rewards for prompt payments, which can help improve cash flow and reduce the gap between billing and payments.

Forecasting for Maintenance and Unplanned Costs

As a Utilities and Energy company, you are responsible for providing essential services to your customers. This means that you must be prepared for unexpected maintenance or repair costs that can arise at any time. These costs can significantly impact your cash flow and disrupt your operations if not properly planned for. To effectively manage these costs, it is crucial to include them in your cash flow forecast. This means setting aside a portion of your budget for maintenance and unplanned expenses. It's always better to be over-prepared than under-prepared when it comes to unexpected costs. Another strategy is to create an emergency fund specifically for unplanned costs. This can help cover any unexpected expenses without disrupting your overall cash flow. Having a backup plan in place can provide peace of mind and ensure that your company can continue to operate smoothly.

Strategies for Mitigating Risks

The Utilities and Energy industry is highly regulated and subject to changes in government policies and regulations. These changes can have a significant impact on your cash flow and overall business operations. To mitigate these risks, it is crucial to stay updated on industry regulations and policies and include any potential changes in your cash flow forecasting. Another risk that Utilities and Energy companies face is the fluctuation of energy prices. Changes in energy prices can affect not only your revenue but also your expenses. It's important to carefully monitor and analyze energy prices and make necessary adjustments to your cash flow forecast to ensure that you are prepared for any potential changes. Another helpful strategy is to diversify your revenue streams. This can provide a more stable cash flow and mitigate the risks associated with relying on a single source of income.

In conclusion, cash flow forecasting in Utilities and Energy companies requires careful planning and analysis. By managing timing differences in billing and payments, forecasting for maintenance and unplanned costs, and mitigating risks, you can ensure a steady and reliable cash flow for your business. Stay informed, be prepared, and always have a backup plan in place to protect your company's financial stability.

Made in United States
Orlando, FL
05 March 2024

44416736R00075